BAD FOR THE JEWS

Also by Scott Sherman

The New Vampires Handbook: A Guide for the Recently Turned Creature of the Night
with Joe Garden, Janet Ginsburg, Chris Pauls, Anita Serwacki

The Dangerous Book for Dogs

The Devious Book for Cats

THOMAS DUNNE BOOKS.
An imprint of St. Martin's Press.

www.thomasdunnebooks.com
www.stmartins.com

ISBN 978-0-312-66845-7

First Edition: September 2011

10 9 8 7 6 5 4 3 2 1

BAD FOR THE JEWS

Scott Sherman

Thomas Dunne Books
St. Martin's Griffin
New York

To Mom and Dad,
Thanks for the Faith!

CONTENTS

INTRODUCTION

Let's get the obvious out of the way first. Making a list of Jews is generally a bad thing to do. Honestly, I don't know how God did it when He wrote the Book of Life. The writing process must've been hellacious. I do wonder, after writing *Bad for the Jews,* how many times He thought, "Do I include Jake Gyllenhaal? He seems like a good boy. Not a bad actor. On the other hand, there's just something about him that really gets under my skin." I don't even want to know how many sins against Yahweh I just committed by trying to know His thoughts, assuming His thoughts include references to Jake Gyllenhaal and, just at the beginning of this sentence, spelling His name with vowels. The Book of Life notwithstanding, there's really no list of Jews written by non-Jews here on Earth that has turned out to be a good thing for us. Even setting aside lists of Teutonic origin, it's hard to imagine too many cases in which somebody who isn't Jewish would write down names of Jews for noble and innocent purposes. And don't say, "What about Hollywood power lists?" If the name Tom Cruise appears on a list, it's not kosher. I'm reasonably certain there's a halakhic law about that.

A Christian friend and frequent collaborator of mine does, in fact, keep a written list, in a chunky red notepad, of Jews he's met. There's a doodled Star of David on the cover. It's actually kind of cute, and it's the only exception to the rule that I know of. I can say with complete confidence that he keeps his list with the best of intentions. There are very very few Jews who live in his community, and as an adult he began to wonder if he had even met any Jews. To his credit, he did not want to assume by looks, mannerisms, or thriftiness that anybody he knew was of Hebraic stock. In order to make the list, a Jew would have to identify him- or herself as such, and—here's the twist—do so without any prompting. The Moshiach could sit down in my friend's living room, break bread, and ask for three sugar cubes in his tea, but if he did not explicitly declare that he was the Jewish Messiah, he would not make the list.

I feel honored to be in that notepad. It's documentation that I am not shy about my Judaism. At some point, apropos of nothing, I let him know I was Jewish. That wasn't always the case. I have lived in parts of America where, as a Jew, I was the diversity. After my bar mitzvah, a friend asked me if Jews were Chicago Bears fans "or something." It took several confusing exchanges before I realized every time I said Adonai, he heard Illinois. That's the kind of conversation that makes you think mentioning your minority-status religion isn't worth the trouble. Nothing anti-Semitic about it, mind you, but a huge pain in the ass as far as discourse goes.

At that same bar mitzvah, I was introduced to lists of Jews with whom many many thirteen-year-olds find themselves involuntarily acquainted: Great Jews. Since the older members of our small congregation only knew of me as the kid who liked to perform, I received five copies of Darryl Lyman's *Great Jews on Stage and Screen.* Rest assured, had I not prematurely ended my competitive sports career after injuring myself putting on a T-ball uniform, I would have most certainly been inundated with books of famous Jewish athletes.

I would go so far as to say that Jews sharing lists of great Jews with other Jews is part of both the scholarly and the social tradition. I wasn't awake to see the *Saturday Night Live* episode in which Adam Sandler sang "The Hanukkah Song," but you know when I did see it? The next morning at Hebrew school when the teachers herded all the kids in the synagogue into the all-purpose room to watch a recording of it, which was promptly followed by the distribution of the lyrics to the song, which was promptly followed by a huge sing-along. The message from

Sandler and the teachers at Temple Emanuel was pretty damn clear: Despite being only a minuscule part of this country, Jews can be great at anything. It's heartwarming, it's uplifting, and unfortunately, too true, because sometimes Jews are really great at being really bad.

And when a Jew is bad, it's bad for the Jews. That's the problem with being a tiny portion of a country—hell, the world. A Christian or a Muslim does something bad and there's a deluge of counterexamples to show that not all of the faith are capable of the same misdeeds. But when a minority of a minority group transgresses, it's a lot harder to convince others that not everybody of their ilk behaves the same way. Wiccans, you know what I'm talking about, right? I mean, I'm sure you can't all be completely nuts. I hope.

A few ground rules and disclaimers about who is in this book. Maybe these aren't necessary to spell out, but indulge my anxiety about being misinterpreted. First, nobody is in this book for being a bad Jew in the religious sense, because let's face it, to varying degrees pretty much all of us suck in that regard. Second, "What about Israel's leadership?" you ask. "Good for the Jews? Bad for the Jews?" That's an interesting question. The answer is yes, absolutely, and no, of course not, but also yes, but let us never forget, no . . . what was the question? Finally, with so many different, perhaps surprising, examples of who is bad for the Jews, you might be curious as to who is good for the Jews. Well, I hate to spoil a potential sequel, but here are a few names.

Larry David. Maybe a little whiny, but the man has valid complaints!

Noam Chomsky. Not what you'd call an Israel-friendly guy, but a Jew in his eighties getting that much love from college kids should give bubbies and zaydes everywhere hope that they'll get an occasional phone call from their grandchildren.

Paula Abdul. Didn't know she was Jewish, did you? There's a great lesson there. You can be both Jewish and a twenty-four-hour walking embarrassment. Just don't do anything that would cause anybody to believe the two attributes are connected.

Bill Kristol. The stalwart neoconservative and editor of *The Weekly Standard* is basically wrong about everything he's ever said, but what perseverance! His ability to survive in spite of his own gargantuan failings should give us all comfort. Jews might screw up in life, but somehow we'll push through. But, seriously, Mr. Kristol is never right.

Jon Stewart. Perhaps you don't like all the kvetching about the media and politics, but his nightly presence reminds all young Jews that it doesn't matter whether you're a doctor, a lawyer, or a potty-mouthed clown, you should always dress nice for work.

So consider this book the apophatic, negative theological, Maimonidean version of those lists of Great Jews. Let's get at the greatness of the Jewish people by not burying but instead acknowledging what's not so great about a few of us. And while we're at it, let's not remind me that a few rabbis set Maimonides's work on fire.

One final note. The Jews included here are all alive as of the time of this writing. We've been around a long time. It stands to reason that there've been a lot of Jews who've been bad for the Jews throughout history, but this directory is supposed to be for in-the-now Jews, and I have a deadline. So to all those who are included in this book, let me say with all sincerity and a little bit of self-interest, *l'chaim!*

BAD FOR THE JEWS

BARBRA STREISAND

The Multitalented Artist Whose Album Is in Your Mom's Car CD Player Right Now

THE MOST GIFTED PERFORMER IN THE HISTORY OF THE UNIVERSE

- Winner of 2 Oscars, 8 Grammys, 4 Emmys, a Tony, an AFI Award, a Golden Globe, an NEA Award, a DGA Award, a Kennedy Center Honors, and a Peabody Award. And she deserves every damn one.
- Has sold over 140 million records. Sadly, that means at least 5.6 billion people are still deprived of owning an album by Ms. Streisand.
- Recording Industry Association of America's top-selling female artist, as if it could be anybody else.
- The only singer to have a number-one album in 5 straight decades, and yet the woman doesn't look a day over . . . let's say forty-two.
- Established the Streisand Foundation to fund a wide range of social, civil, and environmental programs. If she were a Catholic, she'd already be Saint Barbra.

BUT NOBODY'S *THAT* GIFTED

- Convinces fans to shell out thousands of dollars for farewell tours, then proceeds to do a comeback tour. What, you think we're made of money?
- Mere presence convinces every untalented Jew to believe they can become a star.
- Too much with the politicking! Who elected you?

- All those hiatuses. You know some of us have to work for a living.
- The nails. Can we please get those under control, Barbra?

She stands proud, the gilded streaks in her hair framing every angle of her ageless Jewish countenance. With the faintest warble, her legions of fans snap to attention, their rivers of happy tears symbols of allegiance unmatched since horsehair-crested helmets graced Trojan warriors' heads. She is the Jewish generalissima, the Queen of Princesses, the Babs. Barbra Streisand is bad for us because she is, regrettably, too good. Her talent and drive have inspired two, perhaps even three whole generations of latter-day Jewish divas . . . and they're all annoying. Today, you can see them on shows like *American Idol* and *Glee,* but mostly you find them residing in your home and sharing your last name.

Granted, none of these off-brand and amateur Streisands have risen to any level of Babs-like commercial appeal, but that fact is what makes her even worse. Instead of professional hacks who quickly fade once they fail to become successful, those imitating Ms. Streisand's shtick can't be turned off or tuned out. They're unavoidable and they never go away because, much to our chagrin, they live with us. They are our sisters, our aunts, our mothers, and, yes, sometimes our sons. Think of all the siblings who had to go to school unwashed because a sister's watery, shower-based rendition of "Papa, Can You Hear Me?" took forever to complete. Consider the living rooms monopolized by re-creations of choreography from *Hello, Dolly!* Dare to add up the hours of your life lost to mandatory repeat viewings of *The Prince of Tides*.

Anybody who thinks it's wonderful that so many Jewish girls aspire to be the next Barbra Streisand hasn't spent any time with them. The endless pinched singing, the recitation of monologues from *A Star Is Born,* and the rambling fantasizing about how they will first star on Broadway before making the transition to film all ring in your ears for days. What those who live in a home with a Streisandette wouldn't give to go back in time and convince the entertainer to follow her mother's advice and become a typist. The cause of all the parroting, in part, is because Ms. Streisand's Judaism is beyond contestation. In most cases, it is the repression of a star's roots that makes them so infuriating to Jews, but Ms. Streisand is one of the few celebrities who you wish would tone down the yiddishkeyt and just sing. It's the fusion of outward Jewishness and artistic ability that leads to countless Streisand numbers at Hebrew school talent shows and makes so many of us believe we could follow her path to fame. "Hey, I'm already halfway there as a Jew, and I won't even have to get a nose job in order to be a star!" Unfortunately, what is never mentioned at temple, and never will be, is that genuinely artistically gifted people are one of the only groups who number fewer than the Jews.

Faulting Ms. Streisand for the horde of copycats who continually follow her is a bit like faulting the first Homo sapien for every sin committed by subsequent humans, and that's more of a Christian thing. All she did was share her abilities with the world. She never demanded fans to emulate her atrociously. On the other hand, the songstress has a nasty habit of stoking the flames of her fandom with an endless string of farewell tours, comeback tours, more farewell tours, and more comeback tours. Every time Ms. Streisand changes her mind about whether or not she feels like working, a supernova of cosmic exhilaration blasts forth from her star and spreads over the children of Israel. Enrapt Jews race to their phones and computers, their credit cards practically entering themselves into a ticket order form. As the months before the tour kickoff turn to weeks and the weeks turn to days, middle-aged Jews prepare with ritualistic precision to meet Babs. Concert T-shirts are pulled from dressers and children are ordered to play "The Way We Were" on piano. The Jewish world stops spinning on its axis as we do whatever Ms. Streisand commands until she finally once more goes dormant to spend more time barbecuing with the Clintons and kissing James Brolin.

SETH ROGEN

They Put the Schlubby Kid from Hebrew School in the Movies?

SUCH A SUCCESS, EVEN WITH THAT FACE

- Acts, writes, and produces. A triple threat *and* he never finished college!
- Nominated for a writing Emmy for his work on *Da Ali G Show* when he was only in his early twenties. He's like a child prodigy, but for fart jokes instead of math.
- Performed stand-up comedy at a Habonim Dror camp, just like Golda Meir. (OK, Ms. Meir only attended the camp, but oh was she funny!)
- Appeared in six movies that have made over $100 million, which is no small feat when there aren't any giant space robots or dinosaurs in them.
- Characters he portrays often mention they are Jewish!

WHAT KIND OF EXAMPLE ARE YOU SETTING FOR ALL THE JEWS WHO LOOK EXACTLY LIKE YOU?

- Acts, writes, and produces. A triple threat *but* he never finished college.
- Winner of a High Times Stony Award for Stoner of the Year. Are you proud of yourself, Seth?
- So much cursing in his movies.
- And who's asking to see him without a shirt on?
- And would it kill you to keep a tidy beard?

God help any Jewish grandparent watching a Seth Rogen movie. "Well I don't get it," they'll say with a signature mixture of disgust and dismissal before mumbling in their seats, "What kind of person would find this funny?" But beyond their dissatisfaction with the humor, even the most lucid bubbie and zayde will think they're watching their grandson on screen. Mr. Rogen has very niche protean abilities. He can become the exact doppelganger of anybody, so long as they are a Jewish male under the age of thirty.

Now, if Mr. Rogen were to star in a riveting movie about a nice boy who visits his grandparents no matter how much work he needs to get done and never brings up the fact that they never make an effort to visit him, then maybe his roles wouldn't present such a problem for all the Jewish guys he looks like. Unfortunately, Mr. Rogen has chosen to earn his bones starring in comedies about various strains of man-children who only say they're Jewish for the sake of a joke and almost never mention how much they can't wait to attend shul. Nor do the characters sit down to enjoy a large meal of leftover kasha varnishkes they were sent home with after sitting shiva for a relative's neighbor they had never met. Nor do they write thoughtful thank-you cards for the key chain they received for Hanukkah. Jewish grandparents seeing these films in turn project his loutishness onto their own grandsons, and suddenly we're all bad people.

But Jewish grandsons are hurt by Mr. Rogen in another way, namely that he has managed to become a success by living out every young Jewish male's fantasy. A little doughy, unmotivated by any grand ideals, high but functional, sexually active if the mood strikes, nerdy but without being particularly intelligent, and somehow able to get by just fine. In the mind of every Jewish male, this is the ideal form; It is only through the prodding, pestering, and irrepressible call to responsibility by our family, temple, and JCC that this Ashkenazi Vitruvian Man is broken limb by limb until he morphs into the hardworking model mensch that will satisfy (or at least not embarrass) the Jewish community.

How Mr. Rogen carved a Hollywood career out of being the total schlub to which we Jewish men all secretly aspire is a mystery whose origins might as well be rooted in the Kabbalah. This much is clear from his accomplishment though:

He's a bad influence. The notion that Jewish guys could possibly triumph in this world by doing what they want to do, as opposed to what everybody else wants them to do? You might as well disprove the existence of HaShem and submit that our dead ancestors don't care if we study for our AP biology exams. Mr. Rogen, you and your cadre of similarly foreskinless, fortunate schmos, Jonah Hill and Jason Segel, are upending the very essence of the Jewish Man! This is not to say you are doing a bad thing, but it would be foolish to think you won't reap the whirlwind of a thousand angry bubbies for it. Gird yourself.

JUDGE JUDY SHEINDLIN

Constitutionally Empowered Bubbie

SO SUCCESSFUL SHE MUST SEND HER GRANDCHILDREN *SIX* DOLLARS ON THEIR BIRTHDAYS

- Served 10 years as a prosecutor and 14 years as a judge in New York City. A dedicated public servant!
- *Judge Judy* has been the highest-rated court show since its premiere. You don't get these ratings by accident, you know!
- Author of several self-help, judicial issues, and children's books. Is there no topic on which she is not an expert?
- Ranked by *Forbes* as one of the top 20 richest women in entertainment, and she didn't wear one skimpy outfit to get there.
- On VH1's list of the 200 Greatest Pop Culture Icons and received a star on the Hollywood Walk of Fame. How many elderly women who didn't appear on *Golden Girls* can say that?

QUESTION HER JURISPRUDENCE AND IT'LL BE YOUR LAST

- Criticized by judges and law professors as behaving in a manner unbecoming for the court. Look, this is just other people talking here. She seems like a wonderful woman. But who knows? Maybe they have a point.

- Show is set up to look like a real courtroom (complete with a New York State flag) even though it is filmed in Hollywood and Mrs. Sheindlin technically serves as an arbitrator, not a judge.
- Had part of one ruling on the show overturned by the Family Court of Kings County, New York because it overstepped her role as an arbitrator.
- Provides daytime entertainment that is so addictive, unemployed viewers forget they should be looking for a job.
- Mrs. Sheindlin, even though you're always right because you're an older Jewish woman, you could maybe let a litigant finish a sentence occasionally.

Who thought it was a good idea to give a Jewish grandmother a television show in which her opinions are legally binding? In a financial sense, it turned out to be a brilliant calculation seeing as how *Judge Judy,* starring Judge Judith Sheindlin, virtually prints money thanks to its consistently high daytime television ratings. In a larger, more decent sense, however, releasing the wrath of bubbie onto the world is a cruel, cruel thing to do.

Jews have the luxury of acclimating themselves to the raw power of their grandmothers. We grow into the role as we age, developing the mental toughness to weather the psychological storm. This is not a personality to unleash upon the unprepared common man. Gentiles need warning systems, underground bunkers, planned escape routes—basically any precaution that would be taken in advance of an attack by Godzilla. No wonder plaintiffs and defendants alike quake in fear before the gavel of Judge Judy. The televised small-claims court only hears cases of up to $5,000, but by the looks of terror in the litigants' eyes you'd think they were facing the death penalty. Little do they know a Jewish grandmother's scornful gaze will not actually kill a person, because death would stop an individual from having the ability to feel guilt.

To be sure, Judge Sheindlin is devastatingly proficient and immensely entertaining in her role as arbiter on matters involving property damage, recoupment of rent money from mullet-sporting ex-lovers, and, if you catch the show on a really good day, negligent pet-sitters who shouldn't have been entrusted to care for a fragile dinner plate, let alone a $3,000 exotic bird. Even if you're a Jew who has never seen *Judge Judy,* you are already familiar with the general vibe of the show. It's basically a Shabbos dinner from hell, minus the candles and brisket. No matter how pleasant and peaceful it starts, inevitably somebody will be ordered to look grandma in the eye and listen as she tells you in what way you've screwed up. And let there be no doubt that she will be both direct and specific.

Even though Jews are naturally well-equipped to endure Judge Sheindlin, watching her verbally pummel Gentiles gets real depressing really fast. Yes, at first you'll find her command of the courtroom amusing in a sick, sadistic kind of way. Who wouldn't enjoy seeing a bully who has consistently kicked the crap out of you pick on somebody else for a change? But then, after a few minutes of witnessing the carnage, you can't help but feel awful for the sad goyim sacks now bearing the brunt. That's the signature mark of a high-quality Jewish grandmother: Even when you're not the one being yelled at, you still end up feeling like you did something wrong.

Let it be said without equivocation that if Judge Sheindlin wants to adjudicate small claims cases, tell numbskulls that they're "full of baloney," and provide a late-afternoon diversion for people who are either very fortunate or very unfortunate to have loads of free time during the day, she absolutely should. Nobody in their right mind would ever ask a Jewish grandmother not to do whatever she wants to do, and that includes asking her not to give you a potch on the tokhes (it would only make things worse). But with all her skills and instincts, isn't there something more constructive Judge Sheindlin could be doing with her time?

Maybe when she rules against somebody she could knit them a personalized blanket with "Love, Grandma Sheindlin" stitched on it to show bubbies aren't all piss and vinegar. If showing the softer side of Jewish grandmas isn't to her liking, perhaps she could refocus her natural abilities on another set of scofflaws. We have captured terrorists waiting to be interrogated, for God's sake! There is no one better suited to the task of breaking down even the most hardened zealot. Judge Sheindlin could have half of Guantánamo Bay talking by lunch, and without using any of that waterboarding nonsense. The sensation of drowning is nothing compared to the "bubbie death-stare." Medusa on her best snake-hair day couldn't instill such fear in the hearts of men. In fact, the CIA should be using an all-Jewish-grandmother corps of interrogators. Such a crack squad would have found out where bin Laden was years ago.

LEONARD NIMOY

Nerd

LIVED LONG? CHECK. PROSPERED? CHECK.

- Grew up speaking Yiddish and performed in Yiddish theater. A good Jew and a good Jewish actor!
- Winner of the The Space Foundation's 2010 Douglas S. Morrow Public Outreach Award. Just checking here—The Space Foundation realizes he never actually went into space, correct?
- Sponsored the Nimoy Concert Series at Temple Israel of Hollywood. Perfect for those who like a little "Hine Ma Tov" mixed in with their *Star Trek* theme music.
- Has published 7 books of poetry, written 2 autobiographies, recorded 5 albums, directed several movies and TV shows, and is an accomplished photographer. You'd think he was afraid of being typecast or something.
- Released a book of photography entitled *Shekhina,* which used women in tefillin and tallitot to express the femininity of God.

CAN'T BELIEVE HE APPEARED IN THE NEW *STAR TREK* WITHOUT SHATNER BY HIS SIDE

- A Jew playing a pointy-eared half-alien? Everybody thinks we're strange and foreign enough as it is!

- Directed *Three Men and a Baby.* Ugh.
- Has said that he is retiring from acting and will stop appearing at conventions. But what about all those unanswered *Star Trek* questions that have only been asked six thousand times?
- Two autobiographies? Seems very egotistical, Leonard.
- Many of those women in *Shekhina* were wearing nothing but tefillin and tallitot to express the femininity of God.

Leonard Nimoy is an accomplished actor, poet, photographer, director, writer, and musician best known for portraying Professor Emmett Fowler in the April 23, 2001, episode of *Becker,* "The TorMentor." He is also known in some circles (that include a disproportionate number of Jews) as the son of Vulcan Ambassador Sarek and first officer of the U.S.S. *Enterprise,* Spock. Mr. Nimoy has played Spock in a television series, a movie franchise, a line of video games, a reboot of a television series, an animated series based on the television series, and a reboot of the movie franchise. If the time-travel technology on display in several episodes of *Star Trek* were real, perhaps he might have played the role at the City Dionysia festival in ancient Greece. You might say that Mr. Nimoy *is* Spock, but he has already beaten you to that conclusion with the release of his autobiography, *I Am Spock,* which itself is a response to his first autobiography, *I Am Not Spock.* So let's dispense with the argument that Mr. Nimoy and Mr. Spock are entirely unrelated. He logged more hours in those pointy ears than some people spend with their own children. That should count for something.

The immediate question is why is Mr. Nimoy included here and one William Alan Shatner is not. There is an answer. In his capacity as Captain James Tiberius Kirk, Mr. Shatner was exceptional for the Jews. That cocksure swagger, that love of adventure, that light touch with the females of species from every intergalactic corner. Viewers could practically smell the musk wafting off of his chartreuse uniform. A Jew sitting like King David in the captain chair, carving through the universe and dominating all comers, was a magnificent sight to behold, and not only because it presupposed we'd still be around and working hard over two hundred and fifty years from now.

Mr. Spock, on the other hand, was a big Jewish wet blanket. Every time Capt. Kirk wanted to have a little fun and give the old warp drive a workout, Mr. Spock had to come along with his big, logic-y brain and announce to the bridge why it was a bad idea. Just once we could have been the barrel-chested hero with the cool hair and the winning smile. But nooooo, one of us had to act like the head actuary of interstellar operations, thus canceling out any progress Capt. Kirk made in the endless slog to make Jews look badass. Against all odds, Spock managed to remain a cold-calculating killjoy even in the parallel universe episode, "Mirror, Mirror," and he had the benefit of a wraparound gold belt and a bristly goatee! Obviously, as everybody knows, he loosened up a bit and got his swerve on with Leila Kalomi while under the influence of plant spores on Omicron Ceti III, but drug-induced vivacity doesn't count.

Mr. Nimoy often points out that he was the creative mind behind the Vulcan hand salute, which he based on the blessing used by Kohanim Jewish priests to represent the letter Shin. Great. Good for him. So he felt it necessary to associate the unfeeling, by-the-book character with visible symbols of Judaism. Like he really needed to drive home the notion that hundreds of years in the future, Jews are still going to be the nerds who ruin acts of derring-do by analyzing how our colleagues could have been more productive and minimized risk. What's next? Waving a Torah around while giving a lecture on Kirk's recklessness during a victory celebration over the Gorn? Good lord, man, drop your Yiddisher kop and enjoy the moment! Plus, "Live long and prosper" is such a dull downer. Every time Mr. Nimoy held up his hand he might as well have been saying, "Listen, I have to go, but what we did with the shooting of the phasers and the photon grenade launchers—excellent work. However! Let's not neglect to log those mission reports ASAP. And I can expect you at services tonight, yes? The rabbi is going to say Forefather Skon's name after the Mourner's Kaddish, so it'd be nice if you were there." In conclusion, Kirk rules.

BEASTIE BOYS

Jewish Pioneers of Hip-Hop. Sorry If That Description Caused Your Brain to Explode.

"AW, MOM, YOU'RE JUST JEALOUS. IT'S THE BEASTIE BOYS!"

- First studio album, *Licensed to Ill,* was the first rap LP to go #1 on the Billboard charts. Nothing odd about a group made up of Jews being the first rappers in the #1 spot. Nothing odd at all.
- Ranked #77 on *Rolling Stone*'s list of the 100 Greatest Artists of All Time. Not the highest-ranked Jews on the list, but definitely the highest-ranked Jews who just talked fast and loud instead of singing.
- Winners of MTV's Video Vanguard Award, which is the only MTV award that is actually kind of a big deal.
- Chief organizers of the Tibetan Freedom Concert benefits. They perform mitzvoth regardless of their actions resulting in the extremely inadvisable consequence of pissing off China.
- Winners of 3 Grammy Awards for Best Alternative Music Album (*Hello Nasty*), Best Rap Performance by a duo or grap ("Intergalactic"), and Best Pop Instrumental Album (*The Mix-Up*), so luckily each set of parents can be given a Grammy of their own by their loving children, right, boys?

"ILL" IS RIGHT

- Final concert on their 1987 tour in Britain resulted in a riot and Ad-Rock being charged with assault causing grievous bodily harm. This is why we always tell you to turn the music down!
- "Fight For Your Right" video banned by the BBC. Why make a video so filthy that it gets banned? Don't you want people to see your work?
- According to the Oxford English Dictionary, the Beastie Boys coined the word "mullet," which is almost as bad as creating the hairstyle itself.
- Complaints following a concert in Columbus, Georgia, prompted the city to create a new antilewdness ordinance. Mazel tov, boys. You three were probably the first Jews that audience had ever seen in person and no thanks to you we'll never be invited back.
- Was the first act censored on *American Bandstand* after breaking their microphones and handing them to Dick Clark, saying, "Here's your mic . . . Dick." Not nice. He's a very old man.

Michael Diamond (aka Mike D), Adam Horovitz (aka Ad-Rock), and Adam Yauch (aka MCA), collectively known as the hip-hop outfit The Beastie Boys, have been inspiring Jews to ever-so-awkwardly "kick it" since they first rose to prominence in the mid-1980s. Here was this group of Jewish kids not singing, but rapping anthems about rebellion, partying, Brass Monkey appreciation, and communicating ill-ly. It was as if they were using the nascent musical genre as a way to communicate directly to fellow young Jews without anybody's parents understanding what they were saying, like Navajo wind talkers but with sick rhyme skills and circumcised penises.

The Beastie Boys opened the door for a lot of Jewish kids to get into rap and hip-hop music, but what is interesting is they did it without calling any attention to their Jewish identities. There were no oversized blinged-out Stars of David around their necks, no shout-outs to Moshiach, no conflations of the hora and break dancing. One song on the 1989 album *Paul's Boutique* entitled "Shadrach" might have something to do with Judaism, but you'd have to be writing some highfalutin thesis on theological interpretations in pop culture to make that claim with a straight face. As Mr. Yauch noted in a 2007 press conference: "We didn't even notice we were all Jewish until journalists started asking us about it." They never tried to hide their Judaism, mind you, but the focus was on music, not religion. In this way, Jewish kids felt a deeper connection with the Beastie Boys. It was reverse psychology on a grand scale. Since we were never told to like them simply because they were Jewish, we liked them even more simply because they were Jewish. We acted like those annoying fans who insist we were into a hugely successful group *before* they sold out and started licensing their music for use in car commercials. "Man, you don't even get what 'Sabotage' is all about," we'd say to our friends in study hall. "You gotta hear that song as a Jew to know what they're saying. There's, like, this whole 'nother level happening."

The Jewish factor also helped ease rap music into the household. Normally, blasting record scratches, horn samples, bass thumps, and screeching lyrics would get an immediate order to shut down the stereo. In the case of the Beastie Boys, however, the adolescent Semite could holler down the stairs "But, Mom, they're Jewish!" and maybe—maybe—that would buy five extra minutes of listening pleasure before that excuse would no longer suffice.

So why are these three MCs (and one DJ) so bad for the Jews? No, it's not because some of their earlier songs were a little crude, and no, it's not because one of them practices Buddhism. It's because a few of their aforementioned young Jewish fans went on to become god-awful copycats who were not so subtle when it came to bringing their religion to the rap game. Rather than taking a cue from their mentors, Jewish rappers that followed the Beastie Boys went way, way, way overboard in making sure everybody knew what God they prayed to. It started with parody and novelty acts like 2 Live Jews, 50 Shekel, and Chutzpah. You can't even say the names without feeling embarrassed. Have you ever been at a Jewish wedding in which the best man puts on sunglasses and a backwards hat and does his toast in rap form? Or worse, have you ever sat through a show put on by your little cousins at a Purim party after your aunt yells, "Everybody come into the living room! Abby and Seth are going to do a—a what?—a rap? They're going to do a rap about Haman and Esther!" The quality of the aforementioned novelty acts were roughly the same, and while the shtick is cute within the safe confines of a Jewish environment, it's not something you put before a national audience.

Today the Jewish rap acts are far more polished and take themselves much more seriously, but seeing them still causes an embarrassed sigh. They're not just rappers who happen to be Jewish, they are rappers spitting hot fire about Yahweh. JewDa Maccabi, Kosha Dillz, and Black Hattitude are only a fraction of the dozens of hip-hop acts that rhyme almost exclusively about Judaism, which wouldn't be so bad except that it looks incredibly disrespectful to the genre. That sounds like hyperbole, but think about it in reverse. How would we feel if a singer started praising Jesus over the dulcet tones of klezmer?

In retrospect, a little dash of Judaism in the music would have not been the worst idea for the Beastie Boys. Like a vaccination, the inclusion of some Yiddish here and there on *Licensed to Ill* might have inoculated against future unlistenable Jewish rap because everybody would hear how ridiculous it sounds, even coming from those with high-quality lyrical flow. Now we've got Jewish rap disease, and it's full blown.

JAKE GYLLENHAAL

Academy Award–Nominated Pretty Boy

SUCH A GOOD LOOKING BOY, AND SINGLE, TOO

- Had his bar mitzvah at a homeless shelter—not one of these garish six-figure parties with the tchotchkes and the people paid to dance with the kids and the grandparents.
- Appears in the new version *Shalom Sesame,* a 12-part series for kids about Jewish identity in America. So good with children!
- Winner of a BAFTA and nominated for an Oscar for his role in *Brokeback Mountain*. A Jewish heartthrob playing a gay cowboy. This man clearly has a passion for defying stereotypes.
- #8 on *Entertainment Weekly*'s "30 Under 30" list of actors in 2008 and named one of *Interview*'s 20 Most Beautiful People of the Decade. Young, handsome, and talented. This man also clearly has a passion for making other Jewish guys look like schlubs.
- Despite being Swedish on his father's side, he reportedly stated that he identifies himself as "more Jewish than anything else." We got one!

YOUR SISTER HAD A FAMILY AT YOUR AGE. WHAT'S TAKING YOU SO LONG?

- Hasn't finished his degree since leaving Columbia University in 2000. What, you don't need an education? You think you can coast on your looks your whole life?
- Has been in on-again, off-again relationships with celebrities Kirsten Dunst, Reese Witherspoon, and Taylor Swift. They all seemed like nice girls. What's your problem? Settle down already!
- All that time spent working out. We're worried you're going to pull something, Jacob.
- Your IMDb bio says you're good friends with Matthew McConaughey. You're not into drugs, are you? If he pulls out a marijuana cigarette, you call us and we'll pick you up.
- Seriously, go back to school and get your diploma. This acting thing might not work out and then where will you be?

The existence of Jake Gyllenhaal is completely unfair. No Jewish male should be that good-looking. That's not opinion. That's a vaguely data-based fact. Type "Jewish sex symbol" into an internet search and you'll get around 42,000 results. Type in "vampire sex symbol" and you'll get around 121,000 results. That means there are approximately three times more sex symbols who are figments of people's imaginations than there are real, live, Jewish objects of desire. Mr. Gyllenhaal's abnormal handsomeness is not something to be celebrated. It is something to be feared.

For thousands of years there has been an unspoken agreement between all the sons of Abraham stipulating that none of us would ever get so hunky as to make the rest of us look like we were, despite popular opinion, capable of achieving physical excellence. Let's return to that internet search experiment: Typing in "Jake Gyllenhaal" will yield a number of results, but the thing to focus on here is the "related search" suggestions based on popular queries. At the time of this writing, the second related search? "Jake Gyllenhaal shirtless." People are actually seeking out pictures of a Jewish guy without his shirt on. And not for the purpose of satisfying some weird chest hair or waifish bicep fetishes either. There is no XXX-rated site for hot Shlomo-sex. Nobody is hoping to find snapshots of the pear-shaped glob of flesh otherwise known as a typical Jewish guy. With a carnal drive, Web surfers are cruising for images of the rippled, heroic masculine form, and somehow that search cross-references with a non-goy.

What the hell is this man's agenda? Why does he want to make life so hard for his brethren? We're all going to have to do strange things now like regularly visiting one of these curious gymnasium clubs, because Mr. Gyllenhaal just had to show off his uniformly embossed abdominal muscles. He has demolished the impression that Jewish guys are just genetically incapable of attaining such a physique. No longer can we mollify those who lay with us by saying, "Sweetie, I just can't achieve that kind of movie-star body. Maybe it's a lactic acid deficiency. I think I heard it's common in Jews. Like a genetic thing. There's a name for it . . . Gaucher's Disease, I want to say? But, hey! At least I have a good sense of humor, right? That's important!"

Mr. Gyllenhaal, as if to rub Semitic noses in his dreamboat image, has taken on a broad range of roles and enterprises that nullifies the argument that women need to take what they can get if they're pairing up with Jewish guys. From an action hero in *Prince of Persia,* to a soldier in *Jarhead,* to brainy mathematician in *Proof,* to a quirky young romantic in *Lovely & Amazing,* to a complicated soul in *Donnie Darko,* to a gay man *Brokeback Mountain,* Mr. Gyllenhaal has shown he's capable of encompassing every attribute the fairer sex wants in a man. Add to all of that his studies at Columbia University, his political activism and environmental advocacy, and his current single status and it's hard to deny he's the total package. Screw him. Those glacial blue eyes are going to ruin everything.

FRAN DRESCHER

Sitcom Star Commonly Mistaken for the Sound of a Bandsaw Grinding Against a Chalkboard

SHE SPOKE SOME YIDDISH! ON TV!

- Winner of the TV Land Award for Favorite Nanny, although that's kind of a gimme.
- Recipient of the National Coalition for Cancer Survivorship Writer's Award for her book, *Cancer Shmancer.* Obviously Jews who write humorous nonfiction books are great people.
- Championed the Gynecologic Cancer Education and Awareness Act. She's like a lawmaker, but without the schmuck part!
- Given the City of Hope Spirit of Life Award by Secretary of State Hillary Clinton.
- Founded the Cancer Schmancer Movement, a nonprofit organization that, despite the name, does not try to cure cancer through rhyming.

NOT THAT YOU SHOULD BE ASHAMED OF YOUR VOICE, BUT DID YOU HAVE TO TALK SO, SO MUCH?

- Even though she placed second in the 1973 Miss New York Teenager Pageant, she told talent agencies she won the contest. Lying is no way for a pretty girl to get ahead in life.

- Once went to a vocal coach to lose her nasal voice and accent. That is your heritage you're trying to erase!
- Cast her dog Chester in several episodes of *The Nanny*. Why wouldn't you let other dogs audition? Nobody likes nepotism, even in pet form.
- How could it take you until the end of season 5 to marry Maxwell Sheffield? Five years of romantic suspense was terrible for our hypertension.
- What . . . are . . . you . . . wearing?

You're already thinking about that voice, aren't you? It's ringing in your ears, piercing your frontal lobe, turning your stomach. Like a Jewish she-wolf howling under the light of the moon, the sound of Fran Drescher escapes no one. "Mis-tah Sheffieeeeeeeeeeeeeld!"

During the six seasons of *The Nanny,* Ms. Drescher created and starred as perhaps the most unapologetically Jewish female character ever to grace the television medium, although the "unapologetic" descriptor is probably redundant given the latter two adjectives. For proof, the information mavens at Wikipedia thought it necessary to note that the show was broadcast in both English and Yiddish. Such was the quantity of our people's secondary language in the dialogue, which is a remarkable feat given that it likely alienated the vast majority of the show's audience and left them wondering why the characters were speaking in tongues.

Ms. Drescher's performance in the role of Fran Fine was as tight as the leopard print skirts in which she ebulliently paraded around the Sheffield family home. Unlike some other, less conspicuous Jewish sitcom characters, there was no masking the cultural and religious disposition of Miss Fine. Passover episodes, Hanukkah episodes, episodes in which she pines over a Jewish doctor, a mother who always has full meals at the ready and is able to produce them from her purse—*The Nanny* wasn't a sitcom, it was a documentary. Every pinched word, elevated hairdo, garish outfit, and giddy Pavlovian response to the word "shopping" was a concerted reinforcement of a stereotype that many of today's Jewish women fight tooth-and-nail against.

And, damn it, Ms. Drescher had to go and make that stereotype positively lovable.

Somehow, in a performance that defied all good taste—a performance that should have been in no way enjoyable to watch—the archetypal loud Queens Jewess endeared herself to both her own people and the rest of America. It seems crazy. It does. But the sonic assault that reverberated from Ms. Drescher's lips to the audience's ears sounded like, well, home. The kvetching, the kvelling, the sarcastic retorts that are only considered clever by the person making them, and of course the unceasing penchant for eating were all shrill, obnoxious reminders of Jewish family life that, lo and behold, comforted us.

This is not something that is easy to admit. *The Nanny* was by no means highbrow entertainment. Anybody standing around the water cooler looking to gab about an episode they saw on Nick at Nite surely has a masochistic love of being ridiculed. Half the time you find yourself watching it, you don't even know why. You'll be trolling the dregs of syndicated television and no sooner do you ask yourself, "Am I really watching this crap?" than are you saying, "Oh, awesome, back-to-back episodes!" It's a show you watch when you're sick with a cold, alongside a bowl of chicken soup and a cell phone that rings every ten minutes because your parents will stop at nothing to win the war of attrition that is convincing you to get to a doctor.

It's this curious warmth the character provides that causes such conflict for the Jewish viewer. Given all the horrendous caricatures of Jews in film and television, there is the temptation to immediately take offense to Ms. Drescher's portrayal. Yet the character is so sincere and the actress's performance so clearly rooted in her own experiences that we must ask ourselves, do we kind of like the stereotype? Is there a certain joy in seeing the familiar, albeit familiarity we're embarrassed to have other people see? Who knows? Maybe if we all gave in to behaving like the cliché of the Jewish whining wisenheimer, everybody would delight in watching us. Oh, Ms. Drescher, why would you portray a character who would impregnate us with such inner conflict when all we wanted to do was zone out to the strangely euphonious cackles of your voice?

NEIL SIMON

A Group from Your Temple Will Be Attending a Matinee Performance of His Play This Sunday

SO MANY AWARDS, THE MAN'S HOUSE MUST BE NOTHING BUT MANTLES

- 4 Tonys, a Drama Desk Award, an Outer Critics as well as a New York Drama Critics Circle Award, and a Pulitzer for his work in the theater. And not one of his plays features dancing actors dressed like cats!
- 2 Emmys, a Golden Globe, and 6 Writers Guild of America Awards for his work in television and films. Doesn't seem fair since so many of his movies were adaptations of his plays, but we'll give it to him.
- A Kennedy Center Honoree, member of the American Theatre Hall of Fame, and a recipient of the Mark Twain Prize for American Humor. How does he fit in time to write when he's always winning awards?
- Holds an honorary Doctor of Humane Letters from Hofstra University and an honorary Doctor of Laws from Williams College. And he probably wrote a very nice speech when he accepted them, too.
- Had a Broadway theater named after him. Go by the Neil Simon Theatre and see his name in lights! Don't get any souvenirs though. They're terribly overpriced. Just save the program.

HOW MANY DIFFERENT VERSIONS OF YOURSELF DO YOU NEED TO SEE ON STAGE?

- Quit his job in the mailroom of the Warner Brothers building in 1948. That was steady work!
- Once said of his honorary doctorates, "People with honorary awards are looked upon with disfavor. Would you let an honorary mechanic fix your brand-new Mercedes?" How about showing a little appreciation? It wouldn't kill you to say, "Thank you for this nice award."
- Wrote a female version of *The Odd Couple* entitled *The Female Odd Couple*. That is just straight-up lazy titling.
- 2009 Broadway revival of *Brighton Beach Memoirs* closed after only one week. You couldn't have spruced up the script a little so people had something new to watch?
- Maybe this is crazy, but he looks like he's wearing those signature glasses for show.

When old Jews want to get high, they don't call up a neighborhood dealer to score weed. They call up a regional theater box office to score tickets to a Neil Simon play. The experience is one in the same. For around fifty bucks, they can settle into a comfortable seat for a mellow, relatively harmless, giggle-filled experience that inevitably leads to meandering trips down memory lane. Replace the posters of Bob Marley and *Scarface* with cream-colored picture frames featuring grandkids, and the post-show conversation is nothing less than a blacklight-lit dorm room conversation.

"Remember . . .'member how . . ."

"Yeah."

". . . how Grandma Ethel made us eat mustard soup?"

"Oh my God, yeah. Yeah, mustard soup. Classic. Classic Grandma Ethel."

Soon though, Mr. Simon's work, specifically his famed Eugene Trilogy, will cease to inspire nostalgia since those who lived through the time period in which his plays are set will—how to say this delicately?—stop expecting you to visit. The portraits of Jewish life will transform into strict historical documents, tableaus frozen in time. Mr. Simon's plays are like candid snapshots from a Jewish family's photo album, and while there is nothing wrong with or less entertaining about that, it does mean future generations probably won't see any radical or modern reinterpretations a la Shakespearean dramas. Avant-garde directors five hundred years from now will not be setting *Biloxi Blues* in the Qing Dynasty or "reenvisioning" *Lost In Yonkers* as a meditation on animal rights. Future generations will watch Mr. Simon's comedies and think, "Oh, this is exactly what all mid-twentieth-century American Jews were like. They all made a living as comedy writers and were always coming-of-age no matter how old they were." It's just not true. Many of us are doctors.

Mr. Simon can't be expected to put every aspect of what it's like to be a Jew on to the stage, but how about a little character range, a little variation, a little nuance. God help Jewish actors trying not to be pigeonholed once they've entered the oeuvre of the playwright.

"Hi, my name is Alan Sobel. I'm here for the audition. My previous roles include a comedian in *The Sunshine Boys,* an older comedian in *45 Seconds from Broadway,* an aspiring comedy writer in *Broadway Bound,* and a slightly more established comedy writer in *Laughter on the 23rd Floor*."

The thing abut Mr. Simon's plays is that they are just kinda . . . plays. Simple stories with a bunch of characters, some of whom could be loosely defined as kooky, that take place in normal settings. They are realistic. They are uncontroversial. They are enjoyable. There's not a lot "to get." Nobody is walking out of the theater saying, "Now what was the symbolism of the man who spent the whole play speaking to a picture of Stalin while riding naked except for boxing gloves on top of a replica of a harpooned whale?" Not that these hamish tales are such a bad thing, mind you, but the ease with which an audience can digest the plots and themes of Mr. Simon's plays makes them prime candidates for production, and that can lead to problems. Every year you can find hundreds of theaters evenly spread throughout the country mounting his work. Would you like to know what you cannot find hundreds of evenly spread throughout the country? Jews.

So pity—pity!—the solitary Jewish teen in Dayton, Ohio who would rather be preparing for his driver's test, but is instead auditioning for *Brighton Beach Memoirs* because a community playhouse director demands authenticity and the boy's mother thinks it could be his big break. Will no one save this poor child from two torturous hours on stage, shvitzing and fumbling with an affected Brooklyn accent? We need an embargo on the importation of the Simonian Jew! It's like Mr. Simon is the Pizza Hut of Jewish stereotypes, delivering them hot and fresh to the doorsteps of America. His plays literally metamorphose those of us who have never been considered cliché by our neighbors into stock New York Jew characters. Wouldn't it be better for all of us to let the Dayton boychik be the Dayton boychik? In fact, maybe there is a radical reinterpretation of Mr. Simon's work that is worth pursuing. *Dayton's Great Miami River Memoirs,* anyone?

MATISYAHU

Safe to Say the Biggest Hasidic Reggae Superstar the World Will Ever Know

DEFINITELY NOT A STEREOTYPE

- Single "King Without a Crown" spent 13 weeks on Billboard's Hot 100 chart. He provided over 3 months of Jewish pride!
- Has performed multiple times on *Letterman, Conan, Leno,* and *Kimmel.* He's on TV more than any other Top 40 Hasidic musician.
- Earned a Grammy nomination for his first studio album *Youth,* and we all know how competitive the Best Reggae Album category is.
- Doesn't perform Friday nights out of respect for the Sabbath. Honors his Number One fan, Yahweh!
- Single "One Day" selected as NBC's official anthem for the 2010 Winter Olympics in Vancouver. By far the most noteworthy Jewish accomplishment at that year's winter games.

JEW'MAICAN NO DAMN SENSE

- Admits to having spent part of his youth experimenting heavily with drugs and following around the band Phish. Thankfully it appears he's learned from his mistakes (and his terrible taste in music).

- Cut ties with his managers at JDub, a nonprofit Jewish label, before the release of his album *Youth*. What, Matisyahu? We're not good enough for you anymore?
- According to his Web site, his album *Light* was an attempt to "consolidate three years of learning Torah into 16 songs." How about a side of kugel with your hubris?
- Some believe his shift to Hasidism was only made in order to make his act seem more novel. Mission accomplished.
- Increasingly dressing down for concerts and not wearing suits. You think you're so popular you don't have to look presentable?

Gentile fans of the audio-visual juxtaposition that is Hasidic reggae singer Matthew Miller, aka Matisyahu, often ask their secular Jewish pals about the meaning of the Hebrew lines and Judaic references that pepper his music. This is a lot like asking the janitor at Caltech how jet propulsion works. We might all work at the same institution, but we take home very different paychecks. The uplifting, positive, ebullient music of Mr. Matisyahu is, for many Jews, a total downer. It's a constant melodic reminder that no matter how many fasts we've endured, no matter how embarrassing it was to sing our haftorah portion, no matter how good we were about eating our gefilte fish to make our bubbies happy, we're not as Jewish as we think we are. Culturally, sure, our blood runs blue and white, but when we hear lyrics like "HaShem S'fasai tiftach u-fee yagid tehilasecha," it makes most American Jews realize that our Hebrew training crapped out in our early teens. It figures. Jews, the only people on earth who can feel depressed listening to reggae music.

When not making secular Jews look like ignoramuses in front of goyim, controversy about Mr. Matisyahu within the Hasidic community keeps making those of us on the Reform and even Conservative end of the spectrum feel like the dumb kids in class. Some in the Chabad-Lubavitch sect took exception to the fact that Mr. Matisyahu performed before mixed gender audiences and questioned his piety, while others felt these details should be overlooked because his star (of

David) power elevated Chabad's profile while bringing in donations and possibly pushing some secular Jews closer to the Torah. Then the singer drifted to the Karlin sect, which spurred yet another litany of inter-and intrasect controversies. Meanwhile, those of us in the secular Jewish community scratched our heads like apes and thought it was weird that he didn't wear his fedora as much after his second album, favoring instead a baseball cap or simply the hood on a zip-up sweatshirt. *Was that OK? Doesn't he still have to wear a suit? And who has ever heard of the Karlin sect? They don't wear the furry hats, do they?* The thing is, all of Mr. Matisyahu's hardcore fans seem to know about these steps in his Jewish evolution, and while there's no question Judaism is a diverse religion filled with sectarian offshoots, at the very least you'd like to think your knowledge is a step ahead of a dreadlocked, suburban, neo-hippie atheist skanking in the pit at a Matisyahu show.

The biggest problem presented by Mr. Matisyahu requires mentally reliving an experience shared by many contemporary Jews. Imagine you're in a car. You turn on the radio and turn to a modern rock station. You've never heard the song before, but it's a good one—solid beat, good hook, palatable lyrics. Your head bops along, you drum with increasing vigor on your steering wheel, you even start to sing along with the chorus. And then, as you actually listen to the words you're singing, a revelation about the song slowly dawns on you.

You're listening to Christian rock.

Feh! Those lyrics were just in your mouth! Maybe there's a bottle of mouthwash in the glovebox, some gum, even a toothpick—anything that could cleanse away whatever they put in Christian songs to covertly baptize anybody who sings them!

It's an obnoxious experience to deal with, but Jews in America have accepted that such experiences, along with the annual barrage of Christmas songs, decorations, and cheer are par for the course and nothing to lose your mind about. But in reverse? Gentiles driving along and finding themselves accidentally singing a song about Jewish values and beliefs? Who knows what could happen? Mr. Matisyahu's contrived Rasta patois, just like the chunky barre chords in Christian rock music, masks the obvious spiritual lyrics. When a goy suddenly realizes he's singing, "Ask HaShem for mercy and he'll throw you a rope," the results could be dangerous. We're accustomed to the trickery but a Gentile, unable to see Mr. Matisyahu's payos and beard on the radio, might be so disoriented and verklempt that they drive off the road and straight into a tree. This Mr. Matisyahu is a safety hazard! Please, Mr. Matisyahu, if you're going to sing music inspired by Judaism, for the welfare of drivers everywhere, stick to klezmer.

RON POPEIL

Inventor, Marketer of Wedding Gifts That Never Come Out of the Box

THE MAN IS SO GOOD HE COULD SELL BEARDS TO HASIDIM

- *Self* magazine readers named him one of the 25 "people who have changed the way we eat, drink, and think about food." That's probably meant to be a compliment.
- His Improved Veg-O-Matic II is in the Smithsonian collection. The man makes national treasures!
- Two Ronco inventions, the Pocket Fisherman and the Inside-the-Shell Egg Scrambler, on *Mobile PC* magazine's list of the Top 100 Gadgets of All Time. Everybody likes his tchotchkes.
- Was in the Alpha Epsilon Pi Jewish fraternity. A part of the brotherhood!
- In 1999, *Entertainment Weekly* placed his infomercial for GLH Formula 9 (aka spray-on hair) at #66 on their list of the 100 Greatest Moments on Television. Hey, if it makes people happy . . .

NO GADGET FOR MAKING GEFILTE FISH EASIER? WE'RE SICK OF KEEPING LIVE CARP IN THE TUB

- Awarded the Ig Nobel Prize in Consumer Engineering in 1993. Apparently some people feel Mr. Microphone is not an inspired invention.

- Left the University of Illinois after one year to go into direct sales full-time.
- After selling Ronco, the company had to file for Chapter 11 bankruptcy protection. They need you, Ron! You can't help them out with this indoor turkey deep fryer you've been promising America for years?
- His Chop-O-Matic commercial said the device would make cooking "potato pancakes" easier. Are you ashamed to say latkes?! Say it! Say latkes!
- Why are you on TV so late at night? People need their rest and it's hard to go to bed when you're being so enthralling.

It's 3 A.M. You're wide awake. Goddamn sciatica. It feels like a coal miner is rock blasting his way down your left hip. Screw it, you'll go to the living room and turn on the TV. Let's see what's on. Well, would you look at that. An engaging, avuncular man in a green apron. He certainly seems excited about all the glistening food and sturdy contraptions spread out before him. Oh, now the man is putting two juicy, herb-rubbed, five-pound chickens on spit rods and placing those on to the included platform. "What would I pay for such an incredible machine," you think to yourself upon his command. $400? $350? $325? $290? $247? $193? Now he slides the chicken-on-spits into the machine, closes it up, and with the roar of the entranced studio audience echoing his maxim, sets it and forgets it.

Three days later you're out over two grand and surrounded by thirteen Showtime Rotisseries that you've been brainwashed into believing make the perfect gift. That siren of the sales pitch, Ron Popeil, has a funny way of talking viewers out of a whole lot of money. Over two billion dollars in sales, to be exact. For over forty years he has been the late-night intruder who comes into homes through the television, selling people products they never in a million years thought they would buy. Don't feel ashamed if you've been taken in by this telegenic, latter-day Thomas Edison and the hypnotizing demonstrations of his gadgetry. With honeyed phrases like "lifetime guarantee," "triple-riveted handle with full stainless steel tang," "free solid flavor injector," and the coup de grâce, "make delicious beef jerky right inside your home," how can any one resist such temptation?

Perhaps Jews shouldn't be surprised that so many insomniacs have made four easy monthly payments of just $39.95 (plus shipping and handling) to the company named after Mr. Popeil, Ronco. After all, he looks just like that nice Mr. Moskowitz who always offers the elderly rides back to Lovely Pines Assisted Living after Rosh Hashanah services. Who wouldn't want to enrich such a mensch? But Mr. Popeil is not Mr. Moskowitz. He's a guy on TV giving a spiel and asking for money during hours in which a person is often in his most vulnerable, least rational state of mind. By all accounts, Mr. Popeil hawks good-quality products that perform more or less as advertised, but that doesn't mean anybody needs the stuff they purchase or in the quantities they end up ordering. What kind of psychopath needs two twenty-five-piece knife sets for the price of one? And how embarrassing would it be to give the second set, or any Ronco product for that matter, as a gift? "Here, I wanted to give you this product branded with the mark of Popeil. Now you have demonstrative proof that I have no self-control when it comes to being suckered by infomercials. Just give me a whiz-bang presentation and a toll-free phone number and I'll happily give you my credit card information. Happy birthday."

With the exception of some regional Chabad telethons, Jews don't typically do anything akin to televangelizing. There are a few rabbis who yell at a camera on public access channels, but as far as megachurches converted from old football stadiums and holy men sweating up a rainstorm as they ask their audience for monetary support, we've got bubkes. Mr. Popeil is our Joel Osteen, our Creflo A. Dollar, going on television before adoring crowds and offering a vision of a better, more prosperous life, substituting dehydrated meats and hair-in-a-can for Jesus Christ. The rub of it is, when a televangelist's promises of a better life come up short, it's God's way. When a purchaser realizes they spent their hard-earned money on a Popeil Pocket Fisherman that in reality they'll never use to reel in a thrashing marlin, it's because they were duped by a huckster Jew. There's not a special bonus gift in the world that can quell that kind of consumer outrage.

JERRY BRUCKHEIMER

Producer of Film, Television, and Giant Fireballs

PRODUCED *BEVERLY HILLS COP,* WHICH WASN'T TOO BAD

- Producer of nearly 50 major motion pictures that have earned tens of billions of dollars. He entertains all people regardless of how troublingly low the denominator is.
- Regularly on the annual *Forbes* Celebrity 100 list, and he doesn't even look like a movie star!
- Winner of the Producers Guild's David O. Selznick Award for Lifetime Achievement in 2000, but unfortunately he didn't think that meant he could stop working.
- Endeavors have earned 5 Academy Awards, 5 Grammys, 4 Golden Globes, 7 Emmys, and 4 People's Choice Awards. It is our duty as Jews to question. In the case of these accolades, the question is, "Why, God? Why?"
- Named the number one most powerful person in Hollywood by *Entertainment Weekly* in 2003, and one day, maybe he'll stop abusing that power.

NOW, ABOUT EVERYTHING ELSE HE'S EVER DONE

- Produced *Bad Boys II*.
- Produced *Coyote Ugly*.

- Produced *Pearl Harbor.*
- Produced *National Treasure: Book of Secrets.*
- Produced *Kangaroo Jack*, a movie in which a computer-generated kangaroo raps.

Let there be no ambiguity about the fact that film and television producer Jerry Bruckheimer's greatest offense—one that extends well beyond Jews and harms all living organisms—is facilitating the career of director Michael Bay. If this book was entitled *Bad for Everything-on-the-Planet-Earth,* we'd still be talking about Mr. Bruckheimer, but the focus would be entirely on that point. Not since "Peace for our time" has there been a more ominous string of words than an IMDb credit listed only as "Untitled Jerry Bruckheimer/Michael Bay Project." Pardon the digression. Also, just to be clear, Michael Bay makes god-awful movies and Jerry Bruckheimer helps him do it.

Of all the blockbusters from the cinematic demolition team, *Armageddon* is the only film in Mr. Bruckheimer's canon that he should never have made for the sake of Judaic face-saving. No Jewish producer should make movies about the end of the world. They are 120-minute-long open invitations for every Rapture fetishist in the world to question whether the Hollywood Jew behind the picture was tipped off about any incoming quartets of supernatural horsemen. Really, he could have done less harm by producing a reboot of *Yentl,* and given that he's proven he will produce just about anything (including movies based on amusement park rides, video games, and 1940s cartoons set to classical music), it's almost insulting that he hasn't bothered to do just that.

No matter how irksome his one apocalyptic movie was for the Jews (also, quick reminder: Michael Bay movies shouldn't be made and Mr. Bruckheimer needs to stop working with him), Mr. Bruckheimer's real celluloid problem for the Jews lies in his television credits. As executive producer of pretty much every crime drama on CBS (which is to say, pretty much every drama on CBS), Mr. Bruckheimer has instilled in us the fear of ten thousand nightmarishly gruesome deaths and colossally improbable missing-persons cases. Shows such as *CSI, CSI:*

NY, CSI: Miami, Cold Case, and *Without a Trace* fulfill with aplomb every paranoid fantasy a Jewish, overprotective baby boomer can have about what will happen to their out-of-the-nest children. And for the children of these Jewish baby boomers, the CBS flagships have left in their wake thousands of panicked, endless voice mails from parents instructing the kids to "call back immediately because something was just on the TV that has us very concerned."

Would it have been so difficult to set these shows in places where Jews don't reside in such large numbers? Wyoming might not be the most thrilling location for a crime procedural, but at least every time a Jew turns on the television they won't see a decapitated aspiring actress in a scene that was filmed outside their apartment building. Young Jewish adults are not asking you to stop making television, Mr. Bruckheimer. They're just asking for a leg to stand on when their parents call and yell at them to move back home to Short Hills, Skokie, or Dobbs Ferry. If parents see a victim on *CSI: Casper* spontaneously burst into flames because a meth lab in an apartment below is wafting up impossible-to-detect explosive chemicals, at least Jewish children can assure their worried parents that that kind of stuff never happens in their cities.

SARAH JESSICA PARKER

Clothes Hanger of Stage and Screen

SO TALENTED THAT THEY LET HER KEEP THOSE NICE DRESSES

- Has worked steadily since childhood without becoming a complete mess.
- Winner of 4 Golden Globes, 3 Screen Actors Guild Awards, and an Emmy for Best Lead Actress in a Comedy. In case you're confused, the comedy was *Sex and the City.*
- Member of the President's Committee on the Arts and Humanities. Maybe she'll make viewing some nice Jewish works of art a matter of national policy!
- Has her own lines of clothing and perfume, which is nice for those who want to dress and smell like her.
- Serves as a UNICEF Goodwill Ambassador. Who knows what she does in that capacity, but it's probably nothing bad.

THANKS FOR RUINING NEW YORK, MS. PARKER

- Had her signature mole removed, but why change such a pretty face?
- Got married in an unused historic synagogue but didn't have a Jewish ceremony. You couldn't have just thrown up a chuppah?
- Starred in *Sex and the City 2*, which angered many Muslims with its insensitive

portrayals of their culture. Even more offensive was that she expected people to watch that piece of dreck.

- Used her show to spotlight shoes and fashions that no normal human can afford.
- Popularity led to *Sex and the City*–themed tours of New York. Like we needed more tourists jamming up the sidewalks.

'Jewish style icon' is up there with some of the most contradictory three-word descriptions of all time, yet somehow Sarah Jessica Parker has carried it effortlessly since the 1998 debut of *Sex and the City.* So congratulations, Ms. Parker, for becoming the go-to model for young Jewish women on all things fashion, style, and—most disturbingly—relationships. Not to get all "Save the Polar Bears"–commercial on you, but the number of twenty-two-to-thirty-five-year-old Jewish women who do not own the complete series of *Sex and the City* is shrinking at an astonishing rate. Soon, these rare creatures who are uninfluenced, untainted by the wildly expensive wardrobes, bed-hopping adventures, and moronic love musings of Carrie Bradshaw will vanish forever, and the men who date these women will be forced to live in a cold, dark world where their every action will be compared to some mishegoss that happened during one of the fictional fashionista's romantic forays.

Perhaps it's unfair to blame Ms. Parker for the role she was merely playing, but it's equally unfair that we all have to suffer the ramifications of her portrayal of the shoe-obsessed, intimacy-challenged Jewess, so deal with it. That's life. If she had just stuck to playing Annie on Broadway, maybe so many women wouldn't waste untold hours of thought mentally casting themselves as the Carrie of their group of friends. Jewish women should be a lot more wary of exalting somebody bedecked in haute garments and jewelry. Remember the last time our people started worshipping an idol coated in precious metals? God got a little pissed off. And why wouldn't she stick to Broadway? What an acting challenge it would be to play a Depression-era orphan child as a middle-aged woman!

Now *Sex and the City,* the veritable six-season Torah of modern love (along with the Mishnah and the Gemara that were the two *Sex and the City* movies), has affected relationships of Jew and Gentile alike, but nowhere is its impact greater than in the Jewish-American stronghold of New York. The show set stories in every pocket of New York City (except for the brown neighborhoods, of course), and every time it filmed an insipid dialogue exchange on a new block, it piled a layer of narrative dirt on top of a Jewish historical treasure. Maybe it was a Carrie breakup scene by Congregation Shearith Israel, or a Samantha bedroom romp with Shteibel Row framed by a window in the background, or a Charlotte whine-a-thon in a SoHo gallery that once housed the shmatte manufacturer where your great-grandfather worked. No matter the action of the scene, some of New York's most significant landmarks for American Jews became accessories, backdrops to romantic comedy meet cutes and melodrama.

Have tons of TV shows and films done the same thing? Of course. *The Muppets Take Manhattan* alone fundamentally altered the perception of New York City for a whole generation (although, for those of you who've never visited, it is true that sentient puppets roam the streets). But Ms. Parker's show was so seminal to so many women—again, many of them Jewish and identifying most with her Carrie—that they've internalized the show. *Sex and the City* wasn't watched; it was digested. Those lunching scenes and the four ladies who starred in them are on the brain, always. Walking the sidewalks of New York used to evoke the spirit of the pioneering Jews who made a new, better life for themselves in America. Now you can barely hear those ghosts of our proud past over the clomping of Manolo Blahniks. The city's Jewish tales are being forgotten—replaced in our collective consciousness by Ms. Parker's scripted flings and galumphing philosophy on all things eros.

BUD SELIG

Destroyer—Oh, Sorry—Commissioner of Baseball

HE'S VERY ATHLETIC, BUT IN MORE OF AN ADMINISTRATIVE KIND OF WAY

- Brought a major-league franchise to his hometown of Milwaukee. A man who cares about his community.
- Winner of 7 Organization of the Year Awards as owner of the Milwaukee Brewers. Perhaps he would've won even more if he hadn't left to take a job he's terrible at.
- Second longest-serving commissioner of baseball. He takes a job and sticks with it!
- Commissioned the Mitchell Report to investigate steroid abuse, which is something he seems very good at acting like he cares about.
- Organized the World Baseball Classic, which is boring, but sort of nice to have in lieu of Olympic baseball.

ANY OTHER PASTIMES YOU'D LIKE TO RUIN?

- Reinstated George Steinbrenner despite a lifetime ban for unethical money issues, but won't do the same for Pete Rose. Set a standard already!
- Failed to even pretend to care about rampant steroid use until 2005.
- Unnecessarily futzed around with the game with his cockamamy ideas.

- Refused to overturn a blown call that would've given pitcher Armando Galarraga a perfect game. You couldn't have, just once, used your power for good?
- Keeps extending his contract despite saying he plans to retire. Give somebody else a turn, Bud!

Here is the short version of the story. Once there was a tribe of people called the Jews who fell in love with a sport called baseball because some of them were actually pretty good at it. With only a few exceptions, most Jews were never tall enough for basketball or big enough for football or dumb enough for hockey. Baseball played to their strengths—not too much running, lots of psychological combat, and plenty of opportunities to argue thanks to umps who wouldn't know what a strike looked like if it handed them three proofs of identification and a diploma from the University of I'm a Strike. Other than the grass allergies, it was a perfect match. Then one of the tribesmen became the commissioner of baseball and systematically razed everything that was good and true about the game, and in the course of doing so, made it incredibly hard for his own people to wholeheartedly enjoy it and even harder to play it professionally. That tribesman's name is Allan H. "Bud" Selig and his retirement from baseball cannot come soon enough.

Mr. Selig's dastardly innovations to the game read like a modern-day Murderers' Row if they were players on a team trying to win the World Series of Baseball Ruining. Interleague play? Narishkeit! World Series home field advantage determined by the winner of the All-Star Game? What are you? Schickered? Instant replay for home runs? Why not just have robots play and take out the human element altogether! Now, these changes under Mr. Selig's stewardship are bad for all baseball fans, but it's especially bad for Jewish baseball fans because we're the schmucks who all the drunken fans in the stands start to look all crazy-eyed at when the inevitable discussion of how much Mr. Selig completely sucks comes up. For those poor readers who don't get out to the games regularly, the answer is yes, the topic of how much Mr. Selig completely sucks does come up in the stands during every single game. As soon as Jews get that look, the need to beat the traffic suddenly becomes a lot more palpable. There's alcohol, anger, high balconies, T-shirt canons, and fuzzy mascots. A lot of scary scenarios can play out really fast.

By far the worst aspect of Mr. Selig's reign, however, has been the league's laughable record on steroids. This utter failure to stop players from inflating their bodies to the point where they look like they should be floated down Broadway on Thanksgiving has been especially detrimental to Jews. How are Jewish players supposed to compete when everybody else is shooting muscle potion into their tokhes? You won't see Kevin Youkilis, Ryan Braun, Gabe Kapler, or any other Jewish major leaguer doing that, and the reason has nothing to do with ethics or bodily harm. It has to do with a steroid's potentially lethal reaction with the most powerful drug of all: crippling Jewish guilt. As a Jewish ballplayer, you know the second that syringe makes contact with the skin of your ass, the ghost of Hank Greenberg is going to appear, a look of absolute disappointment written all over his translucent apparitional face, and tell you about how he almost had one RBI for every game he played and the only performance enhancer he had was his mother's kreplach!

The majors, with Selig at the helm, can tout all the new, stricter testing they want, but everybody knows the end of the steroid era isn't even in sight and pretty soon any player who doesn't bench three hundred and twenty ponds and sport a pair of shriveled testicles won't even be able to make a Venezuelan Summer League team. Soon the Jewish major leaguer will be an extinct species, his competitive drive to win at any cost standing puny when compared to the fear that rubbing some clear cream on his pupik or tushie will incur the wrath and scorn of his ancestors.

JEREMY PIVEN

Portrayer of Jews, Eater of Fish

SO LOUD HE PROBABLY DIDN'T NEED A MICROPHONE AT HIS BAR MITZVAH

- Took his mother to the Golden Globes like every good son should.
- Winner of 3 consecutive Emmys for Outstanding Supporting Actor in a Comedy Series as Ari Gold on *Entourage*. So, despite what his short-lived Broadway career would have you believe, he is capable of consistently showing up to work.
- Hosted a Discovery Channel series on India and shared his journey to the country with the world. And we can assume the next series will be on Israel, yes, Jeremy?
- Currently plays one of television's most recognizable Jewish characters, who is not a terrible person in a couple of scenes each season.
- In an interview with JDate, said he was open to being set up on a date through the site. He doesn't rule out dating Jews! Good enough!

HBO MUST STAND FOR "HEBREWS BEING OBSCENE"

- Has been nominated 14 times since 2005 for his role as Ari Gold. Give other people a chance, Jeremy.
- His Ari Gold character knows about 16 words outside of expletives.

- Says he is a Jewish Buddhist, which is not at all a real thing.
- Failed to think of a nonlaughable reason why he dropped out of *Speed-The-Plow.*
- Seems to choose roles based on how stereotypically Jewish they are.

Based on Jeremy Piven's own choice of roles, it's a good thing the actor isn't actually a talent agent. All of his clients would only star in roles that fit the most ethnically stereotypical versions of themselves.

"Sorry, Sean Connery. There's a great part in this script but the character doesn't wear kilts and hate the English. It's just not the right project for you."

"Brad Pitt, you up for your thirtieth role as a handsome, all-American boy?"

"OK, Nicole Kidman, I know you're sick of playing Australian convicts, but this time, it's an Australian convict *in space*!"

As superagent Ari Gold on HBO's *Entourage,* Mr. Piven wears his character's Judaism on the sleeve of his tightly tailored suit sleeves. He attends shul on the High Holidays, he blames his competitive nature on his "Israeli blood," he co-opts his daughter's bat mitzvah for business purposes and is eviscerated by his wife for doing so. Unluckily for us, he also peacocks around his office in a stunning display of hyperaggression, foul-mouthed verbosity, and an obsessive drive to come out the victor of whatever Hollywood game he's playing. And the brutal way he treats his little assistant, Lloyd? Oy, Jewish bosses should count themselves lucky if they don't see a rash of abuse-loving freaks applying to work for a real-life Ari Gold.

In short, the show's producers could've saved a lot of production money by putting a pit bull in a yarmulke and a Hugo Boss suit. Although Mr. Piven can't be blamed for how the role was written, he could have at least had the decency to turn in a dreadfully boring performance that nobody would be interested in watching. Take a dive, Mr. Piven! Take a dive for the good of your people. Let not your talent result in Gentiles thinking that all Jewish men have in them the same rabidity, the same overcompensatory swagger, and the same nonstop need to articulate the current turgidity of their cock as the character you were, regrettably, born to play.

Every explicitly Jewish character on American television has the capacity to become what viewers think of first and foremost when they think about what a Jew is. It's sort of like trying to imagine talking cars with personalities other than that of K.I.T.T. on *Knight Rider*. Maybe there's some talking cars out there who couldn't care less about their drivers, lack stately British accents, and don't always have a snappy barb at the ready, but since most people don't routinely interact with talking cars, there's not a significant basis for comparison.

If Mr. Piven wasn't Jewish, his portrayal of Ari Gold would be more forgivable. We could watch the performance and complain aloud, "They couldn't find a real Jew to play this character? This goy doesn't know what the hell he's doing!" We don't really want a non-Jewish actor to play the part; we just want to believe the character wouldn't be so insulting a representation if a Jewish actor were to play the part. But this portrayal of stereotypical Jews is a continuing motif in the career of Mr. Piven. He is the go-to Jew in Hollywood. In *Keeping Up with the Steins* he stars as a father using his son's bar mitzvah as a means to showcase his superiority over a rival, in *Smokin' Aces* he plays a magician named Buddy Israel, and in the direct-to-video film *Scooby Doo in Where's My Mummy?* he voices a character named Rock Rivers, who probably isn't Jewish, but nevertheless Mr. Piven's presence in the film definitely reinforces the stereotype that a Jew will do anything for money.

The most notorious tale in Mr. Piven's career is of course his abrupt departure from the Broadway performance of David Mamet's *Speed-the-Plow* due to what he swears was a case of mercury poisoning brought on by excessive fish consumption. Given how ridiculous that sentence was to type, it is dizzying to understand how Mr. Piven was able to proclaim that excuse with a straight face. This act of unprofessionalism, however, was the best thing he has ever done for the Jews. Given that his Jewish characters continually show a work ethic that borders on the unhealthy, it was great to see him rebuffing the character trait so publicly and so thoroughly, and proving that Jews can slack off just as well as any overprivileged celebrity. Of all his Jewish portrayals, never had Mr. Piven turned in a performance with as much nuance.

NATALIE PORTMAN

Actress Who Should Be Playing More Jews

NOT JUST A GOOD JEWISH ACTRESS, BUT A GOOD JEWISH GIRL

- Graduated from Harvard while simultaneously starring in films. Which was the true extracurricular activity? Who cares! They both look great on a resume!
- Has acted in movies since age 12. A child actress, even according to Jewish law.
- Won an Oscar for her role in *Black Swan* and a Golden Globe for her performance in *Closer,* which she might have even won without the scene in which she performed a striptease.
- Ambassador of Hope for FINCA International, a nonprofit microfinance organization. OK, she's another Jew-in-finance stereotype, but it's for a good cause.
- Served as the youngest member of the 61st Annual Cannes Film Festival jury. Pretty *and* wise beyond her years.

DO WE EMBARRASS YOU?

- Has only played one Jewish character and says she generally avoids playing them. So sorry your own people aren't interesting enough for you!
- Filmed a kissing scene by the Wailing Wall. Know where that scene could've been shot that would've been even more offensive? Nowhere.

- Equated eating meat to rape in a blog on the Huffington Post. Yeah . . . there's a difference.
- Starred in the Star Wars prequels, which were pretty unforgivable.
- A bit thin.

Jews are not naturally boastful people, unless you consider bragging constantly about the accomplishments of other Jews no matter how distant they are from you "boastful." OK, we're boastful. To that end, Jerusalem-born, Long Island–raised Natalie Portman has been the source of increasing pride for us. Who knows if anybody would have seen *Mr. Magorium's Wonder Emporium* at all if not for audiences made up of temple-sponsored social outings? To have a child star make it into adulthood without completely screwing up her life is no small miracle, nor is it a minor marvel that a beautiful, talented actress would be so open about her Judaism. Add to these twin phenomena the fact that Ms. Portman is a highly educated, opinionated, and eloquent woman and you've basically got a Jewish female that many believe is a myth—one who a Jewish mother and her son can agree on.

With such a tower of impressive attributes, the inevitable collapse was sure to disappoint mother and son alike. There's really no delicate way to dance around the pain this revelation will cause, so perhaps it's best to just come out and speak directly about it. During an interview for the February 2010 issue of *Elle UK*, Ms. Portman said, "I've always tried to stay away from playing Jews."

Take a moment if you need one.

Thanks to roles in both indie hits like *Garden State* and big-budget action flicks like *V For Vendetta,* not to mention the blockbuster (albeit justifiably maligned) Stars Wars prequels, Ms. Portman has become a darling of the fanboy set as well as the critics. Just imagine how proud we would be to see this popular Jewish girl bringing Jewish characters to the screen. No more of this nonsense like when Lorraine Bracco played Ray Liotta's Jewish wife in *Goodfellas.* And there are so many kosher meaty roles waiting for Ms. Portman if she would only be open to them. How about a glossy biopic of Golda Meir? Maybe a sci-fi movie about the discovery of one of the Ten Lost Tribes of Israel on the rings of Saturn? Why not a remake of *Pretty Woman* except this time the hooker is Jewi . . . nevermind.

Ms. Portman's no-Jew-role reasoning stems from the barrage of Holocaust-themed scripts she receives every month, as if there could ever be too many Holocaust movies! The fear of typecasting is understandable, but according to the actress, she gets "like twenty Holocaust scripts a month," so there must be a few in the pile that bring some unexplored nuances to the genre. Maybe there's a Holocaust movie told through the eyes of a morally conflicted, talking German shepherd who befriends Ms. Portman's character, or one about a Jewish girl who learns she has the power to shapeshift and lays waste to the Third Reich by turning into a dinosaur. All we're saying is, don't throw the baby out with the bathwater, Natalie! Considering we all sat through *The Phantom Menace,* it's the least you could do for us.

FRANK GEHRY

Closes His Eyes, Doodles Blindly, Calls It a Building

SEE, JEWS DO WORK WITH THEIR HANDS

- Told by a rabbi in Hebrew school that he had "golden hent." When God gives you a gift, you use it!
- Holds honorary doctorates from 5 prestigious design schools. So accredited!
- Winner of the Pritzker Architecture Prize. And no, just because it's from the Pritzkers doesn't mean they only give the prize to other Jews.
- Taught at Columbia, Yale, and Harvard. Good thing it looks like it only takes him 10 minutes to design a building or else how would he have time to teach?
- Unlike many macher architects, he often comes in on time and on budget.

WOULD IT KILL YOU TO DESIGN A TEMPLE?

- Pulled out of a commitment to work on the Museum of Tolerance in Jerusalem. That could have been a helpful thing, Mr. Gehry. God forbid your work serves the greater good.
- Elaborate art museums often steal focus from the work they house. Give some other artists a chance to have their work admired!
- Why the name change? Prouder of your big fancy blob buildings than of your heritage, are you?

- Designed the bottle for Wyborowa Vodka. So now Jews can be scapegoated for people's wicked hangovers.
- All those museums and concert halls—even a hockey rink!—and not one synagogue.

There's a fine line in Jewish culture between the compulsion to be great at whatever you do and the desire not to stand out or gain an uncomfortably high level of prominence. Work your tushie off and become successful, but not so much that it looks like you want people to make a big fuss over you. Your parents should not only be able to brag about your accomplishments at a gathering, but also feel confident they are the first to break the news. Many architecture critics feel the same way about the craft they cover. Build a sound, attractive, inventive structure, but don't stick out like a two-hundred-foot sore thumb. So, with both these considerations in mind, it would seem as if Frank Gehry's giant amorphous piles of twisted aluminum foil that he goes around telling everybody are buildings are not the best way to go.

Despite some of the professional criticism of Mr. Gehry's work that contends his designs are too flashy, the innovative architect's deconstructionist forms are no doubt admired by many aficionados and ordinary passersby as artistic, boundary-pushing buildings. While aesthetic quality is not something that is being judged here, as a Jew, Mr. Gehry really needs to be careful. First of all, exposed studs?! Are you crazy? Somebody could scrape themselves on those things! You want everybody who hurts themselves walking by your buildings to be a contestant on Sue The Jew?

But second, and more important, Mr. Gehry should be wary of the direction he pushes the envelope. Revolutionary designs inspire other architects to follow suit, but sometimes that's like a samurai handing his sword to a kid who shows an interest in stabbing things indiscriminately. You can't just be nutty enough to try a design as audacious as Mr. Gehry's; you've got to have the supreme skill necessary to handle it responsibly, because in architecture, if that component is lacking, things collapse (or, to complete the earlier muddled analogy, lots of people get stabbed). We'll have to wait a few years to find out what kind of mishegoss Mr. Gehry's anarchic work will inspire, but the results might be a little on the insane side. Hospitals in the shape of porcupines, apartment buildings with no floors, opera houses made of lint, attics in basements—who knows?

Will it be Mr. Gehry's fault when all the buildings on earth resemble LEGO structures that have been knocked over by a hyperactive child? No. Will he blamed for those buildings even though they were designed by shoddy imitators? Probably. Will the fact that he's Jewish somehow be tied into the condemnation even though his religion has nothing to do with it? Have you forgotten what book you're reading?

Sure, giggle at the meshuge author who is clearly stretching both logic and reason in order to have an excuse to write about Mr. Gehry so that he can make his architect mother happy. But consider this tidbit of information, admittedly insightful reader. Would you like to know who else believes a Jew has something to fear by creating stunning and freakish structures that brings him unmatched celebrity in the world of architecture? One Mr. Ephraim Owen Goldberg, better known as Mr. Frank O. Gehry. Ah ha! In the documentary *Sketches of Frank Gehry,* he says the name change came about at the request of his first wife and he "rationalized it as anti-Semitism." Hey, Mr. Bigshot Architect, instead of changing your name to avoid anti-Semitism, why not try making your buildings look like buildings? What, like everybody has to know the name of the shmendrik who designed the place they're standing in? Oy, the ego on you!

JERRY SEINFELD

A Jew About Nothing

FUNNY GUY!

- Creator, writer, producer, and star of a show with his own name as its title. A little egomaniacal, but otherwise spectacular!
- Worked on an Israeli kibbutz in 1970. It must have been *fertile ground* for comedy! Zing! Hello! Is this thing on?
- Was the subject of the 2002 documentary *Comedian,* which finally did away with the idea that all documentaries about Jews had to be about World War II.
- Kept his fictional apartment very tidy without his mother ever having to ask.
- In 2009, was #37 on *Forbes* Celebrity 100 list, and he barely even did anything that year!

HEY, MR. OBSERVATIONAL HUMOR, WHY NOT TRY OBSERVING THE SABBATH, EH?

- Sued for defamation after publicly insulting an author who accused his wife of plagiarism. You think just because you're so funny you can be mean? What kind of sick Jewish writer would do such a thing?
- Was the first guest on *The Jay Leno Show,* which almost ruined all of television forever.

- Inspired a generation of hack comedians to start every joke with "What is the deal with . . ."
- Credits Scientology with helping his communication skills. No more on the subject will be said because those people are terrifying.
- 9 seasons on the air and not 1 cheesy holiday episode in which the miracle of Hanukkah is retold in a wacky, yet heartwarming style. Jews don't deserve a lame holiday TV show, too?

For millions of people, Jerry Seinfeld isn't a guy who they know is Jewish, he is the only guy who they know is Jewish. Throughout the nineties, Mr. Seinfeld's eponymous sitcom became the biggest cultural touchstone since the early first-century talk show, *Sermonizin' On the Mount with Jesus H. Christ,* and as the popularity of *Seinfeld* rose, the comedian at the center of it became as equally well-known a Jew as the aforementioned show host. Unfortunately, as with Jesus, Mr. Seinfeld did nothing to improve our image.

Is it too much to ask that the most popular Jew on the planet use his platform for our benefit? Probably. On the other hand, it's a reasonable trade-off considering that because of his popularity there is a bloc of people out there who think mass cereal consumption is a part of everyday Jewish life. That's what happens when you're a household name who is also part of an often-misunderstood group. Every minute detail, every quirk, every unconventional action has the potential to be misconstrued as a product of your ethnic or religious background. For all we know, some Gentile fans think never locking doors, always eating at the same restaurant, and spending every waking second sitting in judgment of others are fundamental precepts of Judaism. To be clear, only the latter is true.

Mr. Seinfeld couldn't have been expected to pitch a comedy to NBC about how Jews aren't as awful as most people think we are. Such a premise is probably the only one less likely to get a series than "a show about nothing." But once the show had a firm foothold in the ratings and advertisers where offering up their firstborn for the chance to stick their commercials in between acts, why couldn't Mr. Seinfeld have filmed a very special episode of *Seinfeld* in which, at the end of the show, he sits in a director's chair and talks directly to the camera about how contrary to popular belief, Jews do not control the world, the banks, and the media? The moment could even be punctuated by that infernal animated shooting star and the words *The More You Know*. We're not talking about hijacking the gleeful nihilism of the show for the sake of proselytizing; it would merely be a few seconds in which viewers would learn something from their best Jewish buddy, Jerry.

Failing to take a few precious seconds from Mr. Funnyman's Big-time Funny Show to do Jews a favor is one thing, but the *Seinfeld* episodes in which Judaism is acknowledged directly never failed to ignite a row in the community. The "Soup Nazi" episode made every goy in the world think the coast was clear to trivialize the Holocaust by playing fast and loose with who you could call a Nazi. And besides, Mr. Seinfeld, is a man not allowed to sell soup in the manner of his choosing? Let the man sell his soup how he likes! Who's forcing you to buy this soup? The episode in which Jerry makes out during *Schindler's List* caused every Jewish mother to ask her child, "You would never do something like that, would you?" which in turn caused Jewish children to lie to their mothers when they replied, "Of course not." When a dentist character converts in order to make Jewish jokes, Jerry reacts with an appropriate level of scorn and revulsion, but as he admits, it offends him more "as a comedian." Maybe that's a funny premise, but seeing somebody make Jewish jokes without having earned it by suffering a lifetime of pessimism, neuroses, and guilt is both insulting and unfair. Finally, in the episode "The Bris," Kramer's attempt to stop the circumcision, coupled with a mohel's slicing accident, fomented the ever-present apprehension about all that could go horribly wrong during one of the most hallowed Jewish traditions.

By virtue of the fact that the above examples have not sat well with many of us, Mr. Seinfeld's work ended up hurting Jews in a much more serious way; namely, it revealed that sometimes we absolutely stink at making fun of ourselves whenever the self-deprecating humor is made available to all. If *Seinfeld* aired on closed-circuit television and was only broadcast to synagogues, we'd all be fine with the Jewish-themed episodes. We'd laugh our yarmulke-covered heads off! But since the episodes were seen by a good third of the planet, suddenly we're all on our guard. Is everybody going to get the jokes? Will they be interpreted the wrong way? What kind of ignorant kvetching are we going to have to deal with after goyim hear for the first time about what mohels do?

BADDER FOR THE JEWS

WOODY ALLEN

Turns Out He's Jewish

EVERYBODY COME DOWN TO THE THEATER! ZAYDE MADE ANOTHER MOVING PICTURE SHOW!

- With only 4 exceptions, has made at least 1 film every year since 1965. Not one of these so-called artistic geniuses who never actually does anything!
- Winner of 2 Academy Awards for writing, 1 for directing, and 1 nomination for acting. So many talents in such a little body.
- Writer of 10 plays for the stage, several anthologies of short stories, and approximately 40 pieces for *The New Yorker.* The man could probably write a riveting phone book if you let him.
- An accomplished clarinetist who performs regularly at the Carlyle Hotel and has played at the Montreal Jazz Festival, because a smart Jew always has a fallback career.
- Recipient of lifetime achievement awards from the Directors Guild of America, the Venice Film Festival, and the Cannes Festival. He has won trilingual acclaim!

SO PROLIFIC, IT'S A WONDER HE HAD ANY TIME FOR A SALACIOUS SCANDAL

- Became the model for some indescribably grating impersonations.
- Influence likely resulted in a generation of Jews somehow being even bigger nebbishes than they would've been otherwise.
- Be honest, Woody. Do you really have a movie you're dying to make every year, or do you just want an excuse to stand near Scarlett Johansson?
- You can't make an attempt not to have the exact same title sequence in every movie? Give an audience a surprise every once in a while.
- Oy, the whole thing with Soon-Yi. Look, it's nice that you're in love but . . . oy vey.

Had not the nickname "King of the Jews" already been taken by Jesus, it surely would have fallen onto the slumped shoulders of Woody Allen. For more than half a century the man has been the standard-bearer, the purist vision, and the preeminent persona of the Jewish Man in America. So powerful is his influence, so tight is his stranglehold over the modern Jewish psyche that you'd think by now our infants would emerge from the womb with dark-rimmed eyeglass frames grafted to their faces. The question is, what came first: Mr. Allen or the Woody Allen stereotype? Please excuse the existential tangent, but what if . . .

What if we aren't fleshy, bony mounds of neuroses toiling through life burdened by the weight of our intelligence, or our stupidity, or our fear that we don't properly comprehend how intelligent or stupid we are? Could it be that all the constant nagging thoughts we've assumed were just hazards of our ethnicity, from the over-analysis of everyday minutiae to the emotional internalization of global problems far beyond our control, are not actually natural to our ilk? Have we acquired these traits not through biological, but cultural osmosis? As we rumble along the endless quest to find our place in a world of goyim, we must stop and ask, did we inherit this psychological anvil from our great-grandparents and their great-grandparents before them, or did we simply watch *Annie Hall* at an age far too early in our development? Mr. Allen's career has been so long and prolific that the answer may soon be lost to time. The last generation of pre-Woody Jews will soon go extinct before we are able to ask them, our throats stricken with panic, "Does everything you ever think about have to do with either the inherent misery and futility of life or imagining what having sex with every person you ever meet would be like?"

Is it possible that happiness—and not just "Oh, I'm so happy you shared your pictures from your trip to the Eastern Bloc with me" happiness, but the kind of happiness that it always looks like people are experiencing on Christmas morning—is intrinsic to Jewish life, and Mr. Allen's canon has managed to eclipse our true nature? What if, hundreds of years before *Hannah and Her Sisters*, Jews were considered a go-with-the-flow, gleeful group of people? What if Mr. Allen doesn't represent who we all are, both inside and out? What if he's merely an apprehensive, libidinous, somewhat troubled *individual*?

What if the hours of daily semiritualistic self-loathing, self-deprecation, and self-doubt are totally unnecessary? What if we could be spending time outside? Enjoying life? With a low SPF sunscreen on to get a little color? Playing sports? Not stressing about work? Shopping without concern that we're cutting into our unborn child's graduate school tuition? Eating a sumptuous meal without wondering if it'll lead to colorectal cancer? Travelling without the anxiety that at any moment we could be the victim of a hate crime because we're in a country that an uncle once declared, apropos of nothing, was full of anti-Semites? What if we could create a piece of art that, for all its humor, wasn't, at its core, an anthology of reflections on our foibles, fears, and failings? Or have a healthy relationship that wasn't crushed under a planet-size mass of insecurity? Or have a casual chat that didn't end up as a meditation on moral rectitude? What if we are, unbeknownst to even ourselves, normal?

Is Mr. Allen the Chairman Mao of the Jews? Are we just following his lead, marching in lockstep to his worldview, living to fill the mold of Jewish identity that he forged? Is the DVD copy of *Manhattan* tucked away on our shelf the Jewish version of *The Little Red Book*? Would the seven hundred words of this entry, let alone the bulk of this book, exist in the absence of Mr. Allen?

Also, he didn't do us any favors by having an affair with his committed girlfriend's daughter. That was really messed up.

RON JEREMY

Legendary Actor in Highly Successful Films That Somehow Nobody Has Even Seen

NOT JUST GIFTED IN THE ANATOMICAL SENSE

- Winner of the 2009 Positive Image Award from the Free Speech Coalition. And to think how little dialogue there is in his movies.
- Appears in ads promoting pet population control. This would be an example of one of those "do as I say, not as I do" situations.
- A classically trained pianist. No wonder he has such luck with women.
- Holds a masters in special education. Honestly! That's not meant to be a euphemism.
- Lectured at the Oxford Union and many U.S. colleges. A passionate orator who—OK, this all sounds like sexual innuendo. Sorry.

KEEP YOUR SHMEKL IN YOUR PANTS!

- Ranked as the number one porn star of all time. This is difficult for Jews to brag about.
- Has starred in over 2,000 adult films. One wasn't embarrassing enough?
- Not a fan of wearing clothes. Similarly, many of us are not fans of him not being a fan of wearing clothes.

- Chief defender of the porn industry. It's one thing that you appear in the films, but you have to talk about them, too?
- Please, for the sake of everybody, shave that thing above your mouth.

Look away, children. For those pretending not to know who Ron Jeremy is, the man born Ronald Hyatt is one of the most well-known and, in a bizarre way, most respected porn superstars in the world. He may not be Laurence Olivier, but Mr. Jeremy is endowed with an acting muscle few possess. And yes, the acting muscle in question is his nine-and-three-quarters-inch penis. And yes, the penis is technically not a muscle. And yes, your author will move on and apologizes for the level of discomfort that's happening right now.

So is a hirsute Jewish man in his late fifties who has been filmed with over 4,000 sexual partners good or bad for the Jews? Depends on who you ask and how honest they're feeling. Location matters, too. Don't ask this question in shul. Don't ask this question over dinner. Don't ask your relatives this question. Just don't ask, OK?

Despite the taboo nature of how Mr. Jeremy showcases his talent, there is a certain prideful smirk that crops up when Jewish guys discover the greatest professional male executor of intercourse is one of their own. It's a rare instance in which a Jew is totally fine with people thinking what is true of one must be applicable to all. If only Mr. Jeremy had been around during in the Inquisition, perhaps we might have gotten out unscathed thanks to a *Lysistrata*-like twist. "Torquemada, don't you dare force the Jews to convert upon pain of death," the women of Spain would cry. "Without their religion, they might lose their mystical penis power, and then we may never know what true satisfaction feels like!" Sometimes lies about Jews can get us into jams, sometimes they can get us out of them.

But even if you revere Mr. Jeremy's sexual prowess and believe he has fulfilled the dirty, dirty promise of Jews the world over, his evolution from svelte twentieth-century shtup-master to the amorphous, hairy, boinking blob that he is today has to be disconcerting. Have a little pride in your work, man! Not that the profession is being condoned here, but if you're going to be paid to take your clothes off and perform erotic acts on camera, shouldn't basic physical upkeep be a job requirement? Coasting on the girth of your putz is not the Jewish way! You want your fans thinking we don't have a strong work ethic? And think of your poor female coworkers who have to labor under the weight of your belly and kiss that greasy patch of steel wool you call a mustache. You have to foster and maintain these business relationships, Mr. Jeremy!

Now believe it or not, there are some who object to the central premise of Mr. Jeremy's vocation. With a Jew as the male figurehead of the field, many from the puritanical set try to use him to cast us all as amoral infidels. As a matter of fact, Mr. Jeremy participates in a nationwide touring debate on pornography and squares off against the "hip" and youthful antiporn pastor, Craig Gross. Dress that any way you like, but there's no getting around what these debates look like. "In this corner, representing moral values and the righteous path, a mop-topped minister who you know is cool because he uses Twitter and wears an earring! And in this corner, representing the sweaty destruction of purity and fighting for the right to turn all your daughters into whores, a rotund middle-aged Jew! Now let's get reeeeeeaaaaaddddyyyyy to argue about prurience!" This does not bode well.

Look, virtuous or depraved, there's no law against a man making a living starring in films in which he sticks his shmekl into anything that moves, and possibly things that don't. But for critics looking to admonish the industry, Mr. Jeremy is one of the only named targets they can go after without it seeming like they have done a little too much "research" on porn. He's been the subject of a full-length documentary, he's starred in a VH1 reality show, he's written a bestselling book, he's appeared on news shows, and not just ordinary news shows, but local morning news shows. People around the country have casually sipped their morning cup of coffee and packed their children's lunches while porn star Ron Jeremy chitchats on their tiny kitchen televisions. He's positively mainstream. As such, anybody who wants to yelp about how evil smut-meisters are not only living in the darkened, hedonistic corners of society, but also thrusting themselves upon clean-living citizens, needs only to point to the Jew known as "The Hedgehog." Don't we have enough unflattering nicknames?

BOB DYLAN

Preeminent Troubadour of the Modern Era,
Victoria's Secret Pitchman

SO NICE OF HIM NOT TO WORRY HIS MOTHER, EVEN WHEN HE'S BLEEDING

- Winner of 11 Grammy Awards, including the Lifetime Achievement Award. And he is, somehow, still alive!
- Member of the Grammy, Rock and Roll, Songwriters, and Nashville Songwriters Halls of Fame. Imagine all the buildings that have portraits of him hanging from the walls.
- Honored with a Doctorate in Music from Princeton and St. Andrews Universities, a Commandeur des Arts et des Lettres, Kennedy Center Honors, a National Medal of Arts, and a Special Citation from the Pulitzer Prizes. No Nobel?
- Gave all the royalties from his album *Christmas in the Heart* to charities dedicated to ending world hunger and homelessness. Could've had a Hanukkah song on it, but a mensch thing to do nevertheless.
- One of the most influential musicians of the twentieth century, even though his singing voice sounds like he's being strangled by a boa constrictor.

HEY, MR. TAMBOURINE MAN, PICK A RELIGION ALREADY

- In his memoir, *Chronicles: Volume One,* he says that in order to diminish his lofty public image, he "got [himself] photographed at the Western Wall wearing a skullcap. The image was transmitted worldwide instantly and quickly all the great rags changed [him] overnight to a Zionist. This helped a little." The Western Wall is not to be used as a prop!

- Not bad per se, but incredibly weird to see him in a commercial for Victoria's Secret.
- Upset a lot of concertgoers at the Newport Folk Festival by playing an electric guitar. You could have given them some warning before going onstage. Like people need that kind of surprise in their lives?
- Arrested in New Jersey in 2009 for wandering the streets and being mistaken for a homeless man. Clean yourself up, Robert!
- When asked by Ed Bradley why he changed his name, Zimmerman, he responded, "Some people—you're born, you know, the wrong names, wrong parents. I mean, that happens." So we're just rejecting "Honor thy mother and thy father" entirely then? Is that it, Mr. "Dylan"?

Bob Dylan's lyrics are some of the most poked, prodded, and parsed in modern music. Present a line from "All Along The Watchtower" and suddenly everybody in the room has an interpretation, which everybody else in the room thinks is wrong. "It's about the Book of Isaiah!" "The Book of Isaiah? Read the title of the song. It's about a watchtower and various things going on along it." "It's not about anything. Dylan was just picking words out of a hat. He knew his fans would buy every meshuge thing he recorded and then be too afraid to speak up when they didn't understand what he was talking about." As with many enigmatic figures, the discussion eventually gets around to the subject of Mr. Dylan's religion and the role it plays in his music. Here is where Mr. Dylan and the Jews get, to quote the artist, tangled up.

This much we know to be true. Maybe. Mr. Dylan, born Robert Zimmerman, was brought up in a Jewish home in Hibbing, Minnesota, and had a bar mitzvah in the town's only synagogue. Given the Dylan-like mumbling it takes some thirteen-year-olds to get through a Torah portion, the ceremony of the then Mr. Zimmerman shouldn't be too difficult to imagine. As a musician, occasionally he would sprinkle some Old Testament boogie-woogie into his songs, most notably mentioning the story of Abraham in "Highway 61 Revisited," but nobody was calling the man a rabbinical scholar. Around the late 1970s, he sauntered his way down the path of Jesus, which, suffice it to say, doesn't jive with Judaism (no matter what a pamphlet handed to you by a Jew-For-Jesus in the bowels of the Times Square–42nd Street station says).

The subject of Jews converting out of the faith is a touchy one, so let's address it with no tact whatsoever. It stings like a bitch. Nobody likes seeing an ex in the embrace of another, even if the relationship with the former flame wasn't too serious. All you can do is say some cliche line like, "I just want you to be happy, and if that means not being with me, so be it," and hope the melodrama of the moment guilt-trips them back into your arms. In the case of Mr. Dylan's conversion, however, the situation was more like seeing your ex making passionate love to their new sweetheart on national television, all the while proclaiming how much better the sex is than it had ever been with you. He recorded three acclaimed Christian albums, *Slow Train Coming* (which earned him his first Grammy as a solo artist), *Saved,* and *Shot of Love*; he studied the bible at the evangelical Vineyard School of Discipleship; and he refused to play songs that predated his conversion. In other words, this wasn't some private coming to Christ. It was a full-bodied public genuflection. Audiences weren't seeing Bob Dylan; they were seeing the power-ballad quartet of Dylan, Father, Son, and Ghost.

So what could Jews do? The man had made up his mind and, in the process, made some damn good music. No matter the divergent beliefs of those who worship God, Jehovah, Christ, Allah, Shiva, Waheguru, or no higher power at all, surely everybody can agree that "Pressing On" is a dynamite track. But then, just as quickly as it came, Mr. Dylan appeared to lose his new religion by the mid-eighties. The old songs came out of retirement, the exclusively Christian themes decrescendoed their way out of the new music, and the singer-songwriter made inroads back into Judaism. He went to Israel for one of his son's bar mitzvahs, he reportedly studied scripture at Lubavitcher synagogues, and he has been seen davening everywhere from Atlanta to Long Island.

All of which begs the question, where the hell is the trilogy of Jewish albums? We want inspirational Dylan songs, too! Do we not inspire you enough? Are we not as worthy of your incomparable songwriting abilities? If Mr. Dylan had never given such musical attention to Christianity, then it would be unfair to expect the same for Judaism. An artist shouldn't have to sing about his or her religion (and, to be honest, it would be great if some of them who do, didn't). But since everybody else is getting a little sublime hymnal pop music, why not throw your own people a bone? All we got was a little ditty about Israel on *Infidels* and a performance of "Hava Nagila" for the 25th Annual Chabad Telethon in which he only played the harmonica. Maybe if he had recorded a few Jewish tracks earlier in his career, all of his imitators and idolizers of the Jewish persuasion (we're looking at you, Simon & Garfunkel) wouldn't be singin' and ahollerin' about Jesus. And even though the 2009 album *Christmas in the Heart* was for charity, which was very nice of Mr. Dylan, would including "The Dreidel Song" really have been such a chore? Little Jewish boys and girls like listening to you mutter classic holiday songs, too, you know.

JOE LIEBERMAN

Senator of Indeterminate Party

FOR A POLITICIAN WITHOUT A SQUARE JAW, HE'S DONE VERY WELL

- First member of his family to attend college. Oh, his parents must have been filled with such naches!
- First Jewish vice-presidential candidate on a major party ticket for president. Who would have imagined we would see the day?
- Elected 4 times to the United States Senate. God forbid, if we ever have to flee Israel, it's good to know we'd be safe in Connecticut.
- Ran to be the Democratic Party's candidate for president in 2004. It was very nice that he tried.
- Serves as the Chairman of the Senate Committee on Homeland Security and Governmental Affairs. He's in charge of some very important issues, you know.

PLEASE RETIRE

- According to approval ratings, he's one of the least popular senators. That's really saying something. Have you seen some of those people?
- Lost the senate democratic primary in Connecticut in 2006, then ran in the general election as an "independent democrat." Respect the process, Joseph!

What, you think just because you're some macher politician the rules don't apply to you?

- Taken over $31 million in contributions from business and industry. Hard to tell if he's confirming the stereotype of the greedy politician or the greedy Jew.
- Accepted an award from an organization run by Pastor John Hagee, who once stated Hitler was sent by God to bring Jews to Israel. Lieberman then compared Hagee to Moses. Feh!
- In 1995, tried to end the filibuster. In 2009, wanted to use a filibuster to block health care reform. Where are your principles?

When Al Gore named Senator Joseph Lieberman as his running mate, the choice to put the first Jewish person on a major party ballot was probably a surprise to many, but not nearly as big a surprise as it was to many Jews. It wasn't a shock that he was Jewish; it was a shock that he was *really* Jewish. A kosher home, a regular observer of the Sabbath, a constant droopy-jowled mug that seemed to project "I am disappointed in you" even when he's smiling. The kind of Jew that Hasidim might grant is a real Jew (on second thought, no, they wouldn't. But still, he's very Jewish). Seeing Senator Lieberman as the trailblazing Jewish presidential candidate was . . . odd. Just as you wouldn't expect NASA to let a morbidly obese astrophysicist onto the space shuttle until he attained the right look, you wouldn't expect the American people to let a Jewish politician, no matter how intelligent, sit behind the big desk in the Oval Office. There's a basic presidential profile, even in the age of Obama, and wearing a non-Christian religion on your sleeve isn't a part of it. One day, God willing, that will no longer be the case and we can live in a world where fat astronauts and Jewish presidents alike get the opportunities they deserve, but today is not that day.

What did make sense was seeing a Jew as a candidate for vice president. Of all elected positions in American politics, the role of vice president seems best suited for us. Not as much schlepping as secretary of state, you get a pleasant house but nothing as gaudy as the white one the big guy lives in, and every time you talk to the president, you can open with the line, "Look, you don't have to listen to me if you don't want to—I mean, what do I know?—but if I were you . . ." We don't need to make the decisions about every little thing, but it'd be nice to be in the room.

Entertaining the possibility of a Jewish VP was very nice for a time, but thanks to Senator Lieberman, it's probably never ever ever going to happen again. Senator Lieberman has two distinct hallmarks. The first is that he cannot to be trusted in any way since apparently he interprets his "independent" moniker to mean he should obstruct legislation no matter what party sponsors it and never stick to a political ideal. The man is in serious need of some political prunes because he's riddled with consistency problems. As a Democrat, he endorsed and campaigned for Senator McCain for president. Such a thing has happened before, but given that Senator Lieberman was only a few years earlier trying to become the second-most powerful Democrat in the land, it did raise some reliability issues. He once declared in a 2007 op-ed, "for Congress to fail to provide the funds needed by our soldiers in the field is inexcusable under any circumstances," but two years later he threatened to delay a war spending bill if his bill blocking the release of detainee photos didn't become law first. During the health-care reform debate, his changes in stance were so numerous that printing a list of them would require so much paper we'd run out of trees.

The second hallmark of Senator Lieberman is that he's Jewish.

Given these two traits, a lot of his fellow politicians might ask the question, "Can I not trust Joe Lieberman, or can I not trust the Jews?" It's not a rational question, but few asked in the Capitol are. Good-bye, helpful education reforms from Carl Levin. So long, Chuck Schumer's fair-pay legislation. Oh, Dianne Feinstein, did you want that hate-crime bill turned into law? Sorry, since your stubby Semitic fingers wrote the bill, something crooked might have sneaked into it.

Sometimes we forget how close Senator Lieberman almost came to becoming the second-most powerful man in the Free World. A decade of inexplicable actions by the man who almost got the job will do that. No matter what your political persuasion, chances are at some point Senator Lieberman has made you want to down a bottle of Nexium. For any goyim reading this book (is that possible?), if you want to get a sense of how some Jews feel about the senator from Connecticut, take everything you can't stand about the man, double it, make a sandwich, stare at it, and then exclaim you're unable to eat it because Senator Lieberman has made you lose your appetite. Then eat the sandwich a few seconds later because you shouldn't let food go to waste. Hope you enjoyed your visit inside the mind of the Hebrew.

SERGEY BRIN AND LARRY PAGE

Nice Computer Mensches Who Will Probably End Up Destroying Us All

SO GOOD WITH THE TECHNOLOGY

- Founded Google, one of the most profitable and groundbreaking companies ever. Also one of the only companies that still hires people.
- They have won the Marconi Prize, spoken at the World Economic Forum, and served on several scientific and academic committees. Such prestigious achievements for two boys who look like they just futz around on the computer all day.
- Devoted to philanthropic work from environmentalism and education to health and human rights. They don't waste all of their money on customized private planes with special equipment purchased from NASA. Just some of it.
- Have connected people worldwide through Google and given unprecedented exposure to new ideas, many of which are not about the denial of the Holocaust.
- Encourage a creative, casual workplace where employees are encouraged to think independently. And you should see the food they serve in the cafeteria. Everybody gets enough to eat!

HOW CAN WE GOOGLE "WHAT THE HELL WERE YOU THINKING, INVENTING GOOGLE?"

- Both left a Stanford Ph.D. program to focus on Google. You could have been doctors!
- Created Google Books, which allows the scanning and posting of books for free without an author's permission, which is the single greatest crime that anybody can perpetrate.
- Ranked by Privacy International as one the most hostile companies to privacy. You boys mind your own business!
- Business gives Jewish parents all the online tools they need to bombard their children with useless information no matter how far away they live from each other.
- Business also provides one-click access to the toxic nuttiness of insane anti-Semitic zealots all over the world.

Sergey Brin and Larry Page, better known as the Google Guys, have revolutionized the way the world organizes and distributes information, and if most of the information derived from Google search results about the two of them is correct, these two boys should be models for young Jews everywhere. Hard workers, idealists, self-made billionaires, holders of postgraduate degrees. Being the geniuses that they are, they've also made their personal contact information one of the hardest things to find using their own product. This can't be an accident. As the sons of Jewish parents, they must have foreseen the day when their company would endow nosy mommas and papas with the power of computer science, and on that day the first search would be to find out how to set up their beautiful daughters with the eJews.

The degree to which Google has enhanced Jewish parental noodging cannot be overstated. It's not a conduit for knowledge, it's a supercharger for yentas. With natural geographical buffers now helpless to minimize pestering, every local emergency services number can be e-mailed (repeatedly) to your inbox, unwanted tchotchkes—once impossible to find—can now be sent against your will right to your door, neighborhoods can be toured virtually and concern can be expressed about the shifty character on the corner of your block no matter how many times you explain that Google Street View images are not live. If your mother is Peter Parker, Google is the irradiated spider that gave her the supernatural ability to send lists of nearby neurologists at the slightest mention of a headache, or find out about the family of a person with whom you've only gone on one coffee date.

As Jews, Mr. Brin and Mr. Page should have known better. Giving Jewish parents Google is like giving great white sharks a schedule of when and where you plan to go swimming. The problem was big enough without letting them have more information. Also, like the Internet itself, the problem is infinite and unstoppable. At this point, if the guys shut down their creation to give Jewish kids a break from their parents' incessant e-mailing, within seconds the parents will be on the phone asking their child why the Internet "isn't working." There's no solution. Don't even try to google one.

Yeah, yeah, information should be free and accessible to all no matter how incredibly annoying the consequences. Fine. Agreed. Jewish kids have endured the hassling of their parents for thousands of years and they'll continue to do so no matter how the technology changes, because at the end of the day it's better than dealing with the guilt and fuss of asking to be left alone.

Still, it's tough to deny how bad Google is for the Jews when you do a few Semitic-related searches and unintentionally discover that Mr. Brin and Mr. Page's algorithmic beast is—for all its good intentions and remarkable usefulness—a giant hatemonger. It is probably not a shock that much of the half-assed research for this book came by way of Google. Enter the word *Jew* plus just about anything thing in the world and you will find types of hatred you never thought possible. One would think anti-Semitism was a niche of hate unto itself, but oh no, no, no, no, no. There are some folks out there who are postdoctoral anti-Semite specialists. The kind of bigots who get referrals from general-practice bigots. Thanks to the new cybermarketplace of ideas, you can now find out all kinds of new "facts" about Jews. Did you know we breathe poison, cause earthquakes with our minds, subsist on woodland creatures, become ghosts when we sleep, and own the world's supply of oxygen? It's true! The Internet said so.

And for those busy, on-the-go anti-Semites who don't have the time to build whole searchable Web sites devoted to the hatred of Jews, Google-owned services like YouTube and Blogger have ample space for snappy comments and blog posts from people who just wanted to let everybody know that all Jews should eat shit and die for no reason in particular. So go ahead and post clips from your son's bar mitzvah! The racist assbrains of the Google universe can't wait to give you and anybody who views the video their thoughts on the ceremony.

PATTI STANGER

Matchmaker for Monied, Emotionally Stunted Man-Children

SHE MUST BE ASKED TO SIGN KETUBAHS ALL THE TIME

- A self-proclaimed third-generation matchmaker. Tradition!
- Tries to help others (specifically, millionaires) find love (for an exorbitant fee). Who could argue with such a noble goal?
- Keeps busy with a TV show—Bravo's *The Millionaire Matchmaker*—books, a radio show, a blog, and a thriving business. Where does she ever find the time for shameless self-promotion?
- Seems to have very clean hair.
- Doesn't allow "gold diggers" to use her services. Strangely, she hasn't considered changing the entire premise of her business in order to weed them out.

MATCHMAKER, MATCHMAKER, MAKE ME A MILLION TIMES HAPPIER BY ENDING YOUR SHOW

- Charges $25,000 per year for male millionaires and $50,000 per year for female millionaires. It's highly unfair to charge men and women different prices considering anybody signing up for this service is equally stupid.
- Charges $600 per hour for phone consultations with nonmillionaires. For $5.95 per minute, people could just call a psychic and ask them the name of

the person they're supposed to be with. Chances are they'll get the same result, bubkes.
- Specializes in pairing horrible people with terrible people.
- Ostensibly tells women seeking the love of a millionaire to whore it up in the looks department. To be fair, she does seem to mean a very classy, high-priced whore.
- Is in no way professionally accredited to suggest behavior modification. You might as well get dating advice from your mother, who, by the way, will tell you who to date for free.

Patti Stanger is a walking medley of all the worst parts of *Fiddler on the Roof*. Thanks to countless high-school productions of said musical that have been cast entirely with Gentiles, the prattling matchmaker has earned a place in the trinity of Jewish female stereotypes, right beside the J.A.P. and the Mother. So how could this stereotype possibly get any worse? Oh! Of course! Dump mountains of money (and the lust for it) into the mix. Yes, that should confirm every negative opinion of Jewish women that runs through the brain of *The Millionaire Matchmaker* audience.

According to her official biography, "Patti realized that busy, upscale men simply didn't have the time to go looking for a relationship, weren't meeting the kind of women that they dreamed about, or were looking for a certain 'type' that they couldn't find. These men needed a service where they could be introduced to exceptionally beautiful women in a relaxing, discreet, and confidential manner." No need to read between the lines. It's a pretty airtight description, assuming you're describing a bordello.

The obvious conceit of Ms. Stanger's show on Bravo is to pair wealthy, largely inept men (and the occasional woman) with one of her company's thirty-thousand-member database of single, singularly money-minded members. To assume the intentions of either millionaire or plebeian candidate are anything less than 100 percent nausea-inducing is ridiculous. The rich dudes want hot girlfriends, the hot chicks want rich boyfriends. For all their similarly queasy themes, at least recent dating shows like *The Bachelor* or even *Flavor of Love* weren't so brash as to mandate the socioeconomic statuses of their contestants. It has to be a bad sign for your matchmaking business if Flavor Flav is using more dignified criteria to find a mate, right? Yet Ms. Stanger, Yenta to the Yucky, feels that first comes finance, then comes love.

Look, the concept of marrying up, moneywise, is nothing new, but do the Jews really need to steal the mantle from British Regency families? Ms. Stanger could've made almost any other superficial standard her focus and it would've been better for the Jews. The Masochist Matchmaker, the Megalomanic Matchmaker, the Mutant Matchmaker—all alliterative options that wouldn't make it look like money was the paramount value of relationships in the eyes of a Jewish matchmaker.

That said, matchmaking isn't a profession Jews should be flaunting in front of a national audience in the first place. Ms. Stanger trumpets her third-generation-matchmaker credential as if it were a bloodborne skill—a dominant trait in the Jewish genetic code right next to ample schnozzes and curly hair—and that can only lead to other Jews being asked to do the worst thing in the whole world: setting up friends. This dreadful social practice is arduous and awkward enough without the perception that, as a Jew, you're some kind of love wizard with bottles of magical relationship potion to spare. Formal Jewish matchmaking, the practice of shidduch, is a small part of an even smaller part of Jewish culture, but given the attention it receives, you'd think every Jewish woman became a professional shadchan upon reaching puberty. As any Jew who has ever been forced by his or her mother to go on dates with the offspring of the ladies in her bridge club knows, this natural matchmaking acuity is more fiction than fact.

The front-and-center nature of Ms. Stanger in the show might be the worst part of all for Jews. She's not just a sideline host of a dating show, she hand selects the pairings. Our people have a unique ability to attract the attention of conspiracy theorists, and after watching Ms. Stanger interview potential geishas (sorry, potential soulmates) for her millionaire clients, it's hard to fault any wackjob for thinking there is a new Zionist plot to bring chaos and destruction to the world by getting awful people to breed. It's like the missing twenty-fifth chapter of *The Protocols of the Elders of Zion.* Chapter 25: Elevate The Jewry Caste by Making Shitheads Hump.

HOWARD STERN

King of All Self-Deluded Proclamations
About Media Dominance

AT LEAST HE'S A GOOD CONVERSATIONALIST

- Signed an unprecedented $500 million contract with Sirius Satellite Radio. A Jew's voice can be heard in space!
- Book *Private Parts* was #1 on both *The New York Times* and *Publishers Weekly* bestseller list in its first week. Imagine how many people read their first book ever because of him.
- Briefly ran for governor of New York. He doesn't just complain about government, he takes action! Albeit as a publicity stunt.
- Winner of a Blockbuster Entertainment Award for Favorite Male Newcomer for his performance in the movie *Private Parts*. That's right. *The* Blockbuster Entertainment Award.
- An avid chess player, so clearly he doesn't think exclusively with his putz.

IF YOU NEED TO USE SUCH FILTHY LANGUAGE TO GET LISTENERS, MAYBE YOU NEED NEW LISTENERS

- Incurred millions of dollars in indecency fines by the FCC. You think you're special just because you know a few curse words? Don't work blue!
- Has made insensitive remarks about tragedies such as plane crashes, murders,

and school shootings immediately after they occur. You can't sit shiva for five seconds before making your jokes?

- Performed a sketch in 1985 called "Bestiality Dial-a-Date" that ultimately spurred his firing from WNBC. What kind of sick people want to hear that? These are your fans?
- Lambasted and mocked his bosses on the air throughout his career. Like you're such a pleasure to work with.
- Dressed as the character Fartman, he appeared on MTV and exposed his butt cheeks to the world. There are people to this day who cannot get the repulsive image of his bulbous, wan flesh out of their brains.

Many Jews documented in this book are leaders of their respective fields, be they politicians, entertainers, business people, or technological innovators. None, however, commanded the masses like radio host Howard Stern did throughout the nineties and into the 2000s. A lot of times people who believe Jews run the world say that we do so secretly, through back-channel manipulation. We're not ringmasters standing where the crowd can see us as we direct the elephants of finance, the clowns of Hollywood, and the, uh, lion tamers of government, we're puppet masters pulling the strings of . . . oh you get the idea. Mr. Stern, however, has acquired his minions in full view (or earshot) of the public, mostly through the clever use of breasts and attractive lesbians.

Mr. Stern has been labeled a pornographer of the airwaves thanks to his many stunts and contests that cannot be written about here because your author wants to avoid a merciless verbal beat-down from his grandmother. The standard refrain about turning the dial if you don't like what you're hearing unfortunately doesn't help the Jews in this case. Mr. Stern's catering to the prurient interest is so notorious that even those who don't listen know that any given show could feature some of the saddest specimens of humanity vying to be touched by a dilapidated porn star or, worse, descriptions of what the host himself would do to the adult actress if given the opportunity. Thanks to Mr. Stern's warbling Long Island accent, these vulgar descriptions sound like they're coming straight from the mouth of our fathers and uncles. If we did believe in that fiery Christian brand of Hell, Mr. Stern's orations might well be the background noise.

The man expresses plenty of cultural and political opinions—sometimes even of the intelligent variety—but claiming they are the real draw is like saying people who go to strip clubs do so for the buffets. Mr. Stern peddles in smut, but more accurately, he peddles in the truth that millions of people want to be entertained by smut. This truism can be seen in the "most viewed" lists of any online video site or news site, where articles dealing with topics even remotely X-rated shoot to the top of charts. Unlike those faceless entities, however, Mr. Stern is a named personality delivering the dirty, daily goods, and this fact makes him the easiest target for those so-called moral crusaders (not to mention his archnemesis, the FCC). In general, the words *Jew* and *target* should be cleaved as far away from each other as possible, especially when the majority of those mounting the attack on Mr. Stern are, let's face it, not found in any synagogue member directories. There must be some other interesting and less lascivious truth Mr. Stern could explore for five hours a day. Talk about baby tigers and ducklings! Everybody likes those things. Or food! Who doesn't eat? What about clothes? It's so hard to find a pair of pants that fit properly. Why is that? Truly the well of universal material has no bottom.

The radio personality (calling Mr. Stern a "shock jock" feels strange. The man is a gangly Jew in his mid-fifties. The word *jock* makes no sense anywhere near his name) may have lost some of his audience since leaving terrestrial radio for satellite, but he still commands the allegiance of millions of listeners. These avid fans only attract more fury to Mr. Stern. They don't just tune in to his show; they act on his behalf with obnoxious stunts that don't exactly contribute to public enlightenment. Sometimes it'll be a random fan calling in to a national news show and pretending to be a witness to a shooting only to yell out, "Baba Booey! Baba Booey! Howard Stern! Baba Booey!" Sometimes it'll be two male members of Stern's Wack Pack furiously making out while standing behind a reporter on the day of Lehman Brothers's collapse. As the aforementioned examples show, these antics reach beyond the borders of *The Howard Stern Show* and invade public life, often making mockeries of somber or shocking events (except when a notable fan known as Captain Janks called up ESPN during a live broadcast and pretended to be NFL running back Brian Westbrook—that was kind of funny). Even if Mr. Stern isn't directly responsible for these yokels, at the end of the day it looks like a scheming Jew sending out his minions to disrupt the world. He is their Moses, and much like our favorite prophet, he could help Jews a lot by leading his band of shmendriks out into the desert.

DAVID BLAINE

Street Magician Who's Preventing You From Getting to Work on Time

WHO KNEW YOU COULD BE FAMOUS FOR DOING WHAT NOBODY WAS INTERESTED IN SEEING DONE?

- Performed street magic in Times Square for 72 hours to raise money for Haiti earthquake relief. Probably the most annoying way to raise money, but the intention was good.
- Shared his endurance experiences with doctors at the annual TED Conference, where presumably his big health tip was, "Don't do anything I have ever done."
- Escaped from a gyroscope as part of an event to give underprivileged kids a holiday shopping spree. He couldn't have skipped the first part?
- Went to Israel to perform benefit shows for wounded soldiers, troops, and families. A true mitzvah, even if it was a sad ploy to make people pay to watch him.
- Maybe some people don't mind having their day interrupted by a magician who looks like he didn't sleep the night before.

WATCH AS WE MAGICALLY DON'T CARE ABOUT YOUR STUPID TRICKS

- Criticized by fellow magicians for not bringing anything new to magic except for doing it in everyday locations instead of traditional venues like theaters or birthday parties for five-year-olds.

- Took frequent standing breaks during his "Upside Down Man" stunt even though he was supposed to hang for 60 straight hours. Nobody likes a cheater, David, especially when you're cheating on a completely inconsequential endeavor.
- Failed to break the world record for breath-holding on national TV. It's not enough to waste our time on the street? You have to do it on our televisions, too?
- Often starves himself before endurance stunts so he doesn't need to defecate. You have to eat, young man!
- Since when is not doing anything for a long period of time an endurance stunt? Hey, Mr. Blaine, lots of people haven't found you entertaining for your entire career. Where's their world record?

Far be it for anybody to tell another man what he can or cannot do for a living, but if there is one job for which a Jew should avoid submitting his resume, it's that of a magician. Somebody must have told David Blaine this at a young age because the illusionist, street performer, endurance artist—or whatever the hell else he wants you to call him—seems to have a natural inclination to do what he is told is an incredibly bad idea.

"David, you shouldn't bury yourself in a block of ice for almost sixty-four hours."

"Then I'll do it!"

"David, standing unharnessed on a hundred-foot pillar for thirty-five hours might result in your death."

"Let me try!"

"David, living in a suspended glass box along the River Thames for forty-four days with no food is not something that anybody needs to see. Nobody has ever said, 'Before I die, I want to witness an idiot starve himself thirty feet in the air.' Honestly, it's dumb. Why don't you try doing something that could benefit humanity, or at the very least, doesn't cause traffic?"

"What was that thing you said about the floating glass box? Yeah, that sounds good."

The loathsome whispers about the secret paranormal abilities of the Jews have spread and endured; Apparently the Zohar is of no help when it comes to magically refuting bogus ideas espoused by imbeciles. Not to blow anybody's mind with logic, but if Jews did possess magical powers, you can be sure the first thing we'd do is cast a spell stopping the existence of these asinine rumors. What really makes no sense is that an anti-Semite would believe the Jewish people had magical abilities, but would not have a desire to convert. Come on. If there were a religion in which the faithful automatically get awesome superpowers upon enlisting, snagging tickets for High Holiday services would be a helluva lot harder to come by. Other religions might be great and all, but a belief system that comes with the ability to fly, become invisible, or shoot regenerating icicles from our hands? Amen to that!

Mr. Blaine is, to be sure, one of many prominent Jewish magicians. David Copperfield, Uri Geller, Ricky Jay, Israeli magician Hezi Dayan, and, of course, the late Harry Houdini are just a few of the Jews who have been of no help in dispelling the myth that we have supernatural talents, so why pick on the softest-spoken of the lot? Well, Mr. Blaine may be lacking in volume, but he more than makes up for it in the amount of attention he demands from the public. It's not the television specials that are the problem. You can change the channel, and God help the individual who decides watching a nudnik hang upside down for sixty hours is the most entertaining thing on TV. The problem is the public shticks that are foisted upon all who pass by.

Look, Mr. Blaine, you want to do your little tricks, that's fine. Go into the bathroom, run yourself a nice hot bath, and then stick your head underwater for as long as you can, if that's what you want to do. No one is stopping you from doing the moronic things you consider a valuable use of time. But to pull these stunts in places like Lincoln Center, Bryant Park, Times Square, and London's City Hall? Now you're making life difficult for the rest of us. The streets are congested enough without an attention-starved Jew living in a fishbowl for a week and causing every tourist to stop in their tracks. Mr. Blaine, just because you don't have a real job to get to, it doesn't mean we don't. When he performs quick street magic, though, that's when the act goes from annoying to creepy. His "audiences" are people minding their own business who he accosts (often interrupting their meals, of all things!), psychologically disturbs with his sorcery, and then flees from as quickly as he appeared. His tricks run the gamut, but frequently include levitation, elaborate card tricks, or enriching a person through either ESP-aided gambling or making a cup of coffee turn into a cup full of coins. This latter activity is patently stupid for any Jew to pursue. It's just begging for a new theory about how all those Jewish bankers made their shekels through the art of dark magic. There is, however, one trick this Jewizard could add to his repertoire that would be great for everybody: The Disappearing Putz.

GENE SIMMONS

Makeup-Caked Misogynist Merchandiser,
Bassist

HE MUST HAVE PRACTICED FOR HOURS . . . OR AT LEAST AN HOUR

- Bassist for KISS, who have sold over 100 million records worldwide and had 24 releases become certified gold. It's not conducting the Vienna Philharmonic, but still, not bad.
- Nominated for a Grammy. That's almost like winning one!
- Doesn't smoke, do drugs, or get drunk. A good, clean boy.
- Shows off his handsome family on *Gene Simmons Family Jewels.* So wonderful to see the whole mishpocha helping their father realize his dream of staying relevant long after his heyday has passed.
- Merchandiser of KISS comic books, action figures, skin-care products, condoms, coffins, and many other KISS-branded items that fans can spend money on for reasons that cannot possibly be described as sensible.

PUT YOUR TONGUE IN YOUR MOUTH!

- Believes "money is the single most important thing on the planet." Why don't you just say we killed Christ while you're at it?
- Refused to let NPR reair a *Fresh Air* interview in which he came out looking like a world-class jackass. Maybe next time you should think before you speak!

- According to his book, he's had over 4,600 sexual partners, which he sees as totally natural and a completely nonabhorrent way to behave.
- Was quoted as saying Islam is a "vile culture," which in no way is helpful, Gene.
- Gives children nightmares with his demon makeup, blood, sputum, music.

There's a lot of depraved rumors about Jews that would be laughable if the people saying them didn't have the sharp glint in their eye of absolute conviction . . . and often a regional accent of some kind. The rumor that we have horns is a popular one, as is the charming yarn about how we're all agents of Satan. Possibly the most disturbing rumor is that we drink blood. So it would be a real shame if a Jew stood before millions of people on an annual basis, adorned himself in metal spikes, referred to his stage persona as "The Demon," played in a band whose name is rumored to be an acronym for Knights In Satan's Service, and upchucked mouthfuls of fake blood. So thanks a lot for doing exactly that, Gene Simmons. Big help.

And let's not forget what a headache this man must have given every Jewish parent trying to get their child to practice their violin and piano throughout the late 1970s.

"Jacob Hirschberg! Why am I not hearing that violin? You have thirty more minutes of practicing, young man!"

"I don't need to practice, Ma. I just gotta paint my face like a robot harlequin and have sparks fly off my bow and everybody will love me."

"I will not love you, Jacob. I will not love you."

Born Chaim Witz in Haifa, Israel, Mr. Simmons embodies the type of machismo and arrogance that makes Jewish fathers afraid to send their daughters on Birthright trips. He has a natural God's-gift complex that leads directly to his loathsome attitude toward women, which he delights in both professing and intentionally contradicting. Merging the intellect of Jewish philosopher with the alpha-male demeanor of a silverback gorilla is a dangerous combination. It results in Mr. Simmons declaring on the one hand to Terry Gross, "If you want to welcome me with open arms, I'm afraid you're also going to have to welcome me with open legs," and on the other hand to Michael Eisner, "I believe that women should be ruling every country on the face of the planet." Who knows who he thinks he's fooling with such incongruous statements, but let's hope, for her sake, that Mr. Simmons is never received by Queen Elizabeth, lest the "welcoming" results in a major breach of royal protocol. You can't just make up for blatant misogyny by declaring in a velvety Don Juan voice that you love all women. It's like atoning on Yom Kippur by telling God you're actually a pretty great guy and He's just not smart enough to understand that you haven't really done anything wrong.

As an evil clown-faced rocker, we never got to know the real man behind the music, and in many ways, to have left his identity as a metallic spawn of Hell intact would've been less harmful to the Jews. Thanks, however, to *Gene Simmons' Rock School, Celebrity Apprentice,* and *Gene Simmons Family Jewels,* everybody has now witnessed through a myriad of reality TV prisms the unmasked Mr. Simmons, and the unmasked Mr. Simmons is a self-aggrandizing schlock-monster in sunglasses who speaks as if he's a graying lothario on the professional end of a phone sex hotline.

Mr. Simmons acts as his own Jewish mother, constantly reassuring himself that he is the greatest, handsomest, smartest little boychik in whatever room he enters. Upon recovering from a full, elective facial renovation, he didn't reflect on the experience and conclude that perhaps he has some aesthetic insecurities or a fear of aging to a point where dressing like a viking from the future might appear idiotic. Instead, he viewed his face-lift as a well-deserved gift to his fans. We, the conscripted members of the KISS army, have been given the privilege of gazing upon his artificially ageless maw and its accompanying, slithering appendage for years to come. Oh, Gene, why can't you be like your nice Jewish bandmate Paul Stanley and just lay low?

RABBI SHMULEY BOTEACH

The Jewish Oprah, Which We Need Like a Kick in the Head

HE'S A RABBI. HOW COULD THERE BE ANYTHING WRONG WITH HIM?

- Was the host of the award-winning *Shalom in the Home,* a show that aired on TLC before the channel decided anybody who wasn't a little person or didn't give birth to 800 kids wasn't entertaining.
- Author of over 22 bestselling advice and self-help books. Who needs the Torah when we've got *Renewal: A Guide to the Values-Filled Life*?
- Serves as an expert in relationships, parenting, and marriage for Oprah, who is a wonderful woman and it's too bad she's not Jewish because that would be something, wouldn't it?
- Won the 1999 London *Times* award for Preacher of the Year, which is like the Oscars of little-known awards honoring religious figures.
- Founded the L'Chaim Society for students at Oxford University, so we can finally know what kibitzing sounds like with a British accent.

FOR THE LOVE OF GOD, STOP TALKING ABOUT SEX

- Started a charity with the late Michael Jackson that never appeared to do any charitable work. Who can say what's more embarrassing, running a shyster charity or being in business with Michael Jackson (God rest his soul)?

- Appointed non-Jews to lead Oxford's L'Chaim Society and filled it with Gentile members to gain greater prominence on campus. That is not the way to conduct interfaith outreach.
- Gets into screaming matches over the Internet with people like Richard Dawkins and Christopher Hitchens. You're a rabbi, Rabbi! Leave the online tantrums to the brats in middle school.
- Gloms on to celebrities—even that nudnik Jon Gosselin—and becomes their "spiritual advisor."
- Once told a reporter he believes in an 11th Commandment: "Thou shalt do anything for publicity and recognition." The Commandments are not something to joke about! . . . unless the joke is really, really funny.

You know how when you're having problems in your sex life the first person you want to discuss it with, because the conversations are always so natural and comfortable, is your rabbi?

That was a test. If you answered "yes" to the previous question, please get a CAT scan immediately. You may have brain damage.

Yet bewilderingly, millions of everyday Americans are convinced that they should be taking advice on how to spice up their relationships from Rabbi Shmuley Boteach. As host of TLC's mercifully cancelled *Shalom in the Home,* as well as a prolific self-help author, podcaster, and Twitter'er, Rabbi Boteach has become, both by default and self-proclamation, America's rabbi, which is a lot like being China's voodoo priestess. His words on family life, romantic bliss, and lovemaking (to feel a violent chill down your spine upon reading that is normal) have made him the most universally popular rabbi since Krusty the Clown's father on *The Simpsons*.

On the one hand, it is a remarkable and uplifting sight to see America embrace an Orthodox rabbi as a respected thinker in secular life. On the other hand, wow it's creepy. Watching Rabbi Boteach counsel non-Jews is an exercise in breathless apprehension, a domestic bomb-defusing operation that could go disastrously wrong with the most infinitesimal mistake. One flawed pearl of wisdom and we'll all suffer an atomic anti-Semitic explosion.

"I did what the Jew said and now I'm divorced!"

"The kids keep punching me after I fall asleep and it's all the rabbi's fault!"

"In order to 'increase sexual polarity' I wore 'lacy undergarments' and my husband still climaxes before me!" Yes, that is an actual written piece of advice from Rabbi Boteach.

One wonders why goyim listen to a rabbi at all. It's a bit like watching a terrible play that your best friend is performing in. We're the schlimazels who are obligated to attend; why the hell is everybody else in the crowd subjecting themselves to the performance?

This is not to say the good rabbi gives bad guidance, but to sit with Oprah, Dr. Phil, and Rachael Ray and act as some sort of Hebraic guru to the daytime talk-show set is just asking for trouble. Although the rabbi takes pains to say he's not proselytizing when dispensing advice to Gentiles, the yarmulke, the beard, and the rabbinical title all combine to form a giant Voltron-like robot that shoots down any clear barriers between what is explicitly Jewish mores and what is simply his advice as a man of considerable charm and intellect. Do a few well-behaved kids and a couple of mutual orgasms in suburban bedrooms equal the price of inflamed whispers about how the Jews are trying to tell everybody how to run their lives?

Furthermore, Rabbi Boteach links, not separates, his advice to Judaism with titles like *Shalom in the Home: Smart Advice for a Peaceful Life, Dating Secrets of the Ten Commandments,* and *The Kosher Sutra.* He's even written a book called *Judaism for Everyone.* Oy, don't say Judaism is for everyone! You want to get us all killed? Perhaps it's meant to sound inclusive, but that's a title you'd expect to see on a pamphlet for a cult. It's a 5,770-plus-year-old religion, not a group of comet-chasing Windex drinkers, and one of the reasons it's lasted so long is because those who practice it are compelled to do so by their own volition . . . or their parents'. *Judaism for Jews*—try writing that book. It's just something to ponder, Rabbi.

JIM CRAMER

Financial Analyst You Might Hear If You're Within 2,000 Miles of His Mouth

A MAN WHO IS NOT AFRAID TO ROLL UP HIS SLEEVES (IN ORDER TO ACHIEVE A CAMERA-FRIENDLY LOOK THAT SAYS "I'M A PROFESSIONAL *AND* A REGULAR GUY")

- Graduated magna cum laude from Harvard and was the president of *The Crimson*. Such wonderful collegiate achievements, but let us hope with that hectic schedule he still found time to eat.
- JD from Harvard Law, so luckily he can defend himself if he's ever sued for financial malfeasance.
- Brought his family to Israel to celebrate Passover in 2010. No speed-reading of the Haggadah for the Cramer family!
- Didn't charge his hedge-fund clients a management fee during his only down year. Let it never be said that he cares more about profits than people. Unless you really want to say that. There's probably more than a few examples supporting that assertion floating around.
- Created *Mad Money* with a noble mission to educate the public, and, God willing, not too many in the public need to be educated in bankruptcy protection because of his advice.

WHAT, YOU DON'T HAVE AN INSIDE VOICE? SHEKET B'VAKASHAH!

- Bragged about his abilities as a broker to manipulate the futures market by creating "a level of activity beforehand." Yes, that is an elaborate way of saying he lied to make more money.
- Suggested it was a good idea to feed false information to financial reporters, which is illegal but "the SEC doesn't understand it." We'll see if the SEC understands how to prosecute him for it.
- Had Wachovia CEO Robert Steel on *Mad Money* and recommended the bank's stock two weeks before its shares dropped over 80 percent in value. Are you just doing what your shmendrik business friends are telling you to do, Jim?
- Consistently championed Bear Stearns in the runup to its complete collapse, so if he ever starts championing Jews, get nervous.
- Too loud. Please, shush already. Like the neighbors need to know we're watching your program?

Watching Jim Cramer, host of CNBC's *Mad Money,* on television—his arms akimbo, his sleeves rolled up tight enough to turn his clenched fists pale from lack of blood flow, his voice so deafening you'd think the hairs of his goatee would quake off his face—there is little doubt a nation of self-described "Cramericans" are home thinking, "Alright, you screamy Jew, tell me what to do with all my money." Not only does Mr. Cramer sound like he knows what he's talking about, but he's entertaining to boot. Then again, so is a guy walking down the street wearing a sandwich board recommending that Americans take up arms against secret commies from outer space who are replacing citizens with evil doppelgangers. That doesn't mean you should follow his advice.

In a perfect world, Mr. Cramer's vaudevillian investment show would be seen as a generous mitzvah performed by a Jew with an especially shiny head for finance. Nothing stingy about this Shylock type. All his information is free, minus the cost of a cable subscription. Just listen to his Yahweh-endowed business acumen and you'll get rich, I tells ya! He's the People's Jew!

To create such a perfect world, however, Mr. Cramer would have to be right all the time, because the second his advice leads to a viewer losing a dime, "it's all that kike Cramer's fault." God knows the last person you should blame after doing what a thundering lunatic pressing the giant buttons that make the cow sounds on the TV box tells you to do is yourself. OK, so Mr. Cramer might engender the hatred of a few irrational anti-Semites, but, hell, cute Jewish babies adorably napping also manage to up the ire of bigots, so what are are you going to do? Geh gezindt and have a nice life, you Nazi bastards.

Mr. Cramer, though, is not blameless in this case. He calls himself an infotainer who gives serious market analysis in an entertaining manner. This is like a professional hitman trying to justify his actions by saying he did them while wearing a fuzzy red nose and comically oversize shoes. A killer clown is still a killer, even if you give him a conflated nickname like "murderjester." The jocular presentation does little to hide the fact that what he is doing is wrong, and as we've seen so many times, when prominent Jews screw up people's lives, the hate tends to radiate out to all of us.

The instances of his errors are too numerous to mention, but simply being wrong on occasion is not the issue, since the same can be said of any stock analyst. It is, after all, a numbers game. The difference is that most financial professionals aren't going on television every day for an hour and telling total strangers where to invest their dollars. Sure, Mr. Cramer gives every disclosure statement in the book to make it clear that he's just offering his opinion and trying to educate, as opposed to telling you what market moves you should personally make. And all the aforementioned jester-faced hitman is doing is pulling the trigger. It's not his fault if the gun was loaded! There's a reason why doctors don't prescribe medicine unless they first know about your ailments and allergies (no matter how many times you try to tell them over the phone you already know what's what wrong with your body and just need your damn prednisone before your asthma acts up!). You have to know something about your clients. Mr. Cramer is simply shouting stock tips into the wind and picking up his CNBC check regardless of the consequences. That looks damned unethical, greedy, and self-interested, and it sure-as-Shabbos ain't something we need coming from a Jew with one of the biggest, loudest mouths on television.

BAR REFAELI

Jewish Model, Yes. Model Jew, No.

SHE PROBABLY DIDN'T EVEN FIDGET FOR HER BAT MITZVAH PICTURES

- One of the world's most sought-after models, who began at 8 months old. She's like a child prodigy except she doesn't even have to use her brain.
- Appeared on the cover the 2009 *Sports Illustrated* Swimsuit Edition, which sort of makes her a prominent Jewish athlete, too, right?
- Has worked with charities for children and animals including Project Sunshine and Ahava. Both a sheyne meydel and a mensch.
- Lent her celebrity to the Council for a Beautiful Israel's One Bag Less campaign to curb plastic waste. Sure, plastic is terrible. Also, did you see her on the cover of *Sports Illustrated*?
- Winner of the 2009 World Style Award from Women's World Awards. Who knows what that is, but she probably wore something very nice for the award ceremony.

HOW DARE SHE KEEP SHOWING UP ON JEWISH MEN'S COMPUTERS WHEN THEY'RE TRYING TO GET WORK DONE

- Avoided Israeli military service by marrying, then quickly divorcing an acquaintance when she was 18. And what about sharing the burden?

- Justified her draft dodging by saying, "celebrities have other needs." You need your head examined, Miss Swimsuit.
- Attempted to be classified as a nonresident Israeli to avoid paying taxes. Oh, like you're not going to be able to afford your shmattes if you send in a check to the government.
- Appeared nude (except for body paint) on the July 2009 cover of *Esquire*. A child could see that!
- Probably makes Martin Scorsese sad whenever she takes on-again, off-again boyfriend Leonardo DiCaprio away from him.

If this entry was the first one you flipped to, your eyes twitching with ravenous lust after scanning the table of contents, please do everybody the courtesy of at least going to a private place before taking off your pants. Supermodel Bar Refaeli shouldn't be hated, as the old commercial says, because she's beautiful, but the Israeli bombshell is nevertheless a source of angst for her people, and not just because she won't put more clothes on or take more clothes off (depending on who you ask). After gracing the cover of the 2009 *Sports Illustrated* Swimsuit Edition and becoming a household name, Ms. Refaeli achieved something that few of us ever thought a Jew could do, especially on such a global scale. She made a career on looks alone. Modeling might be a highly developed skill, but with that face, what job couldn't she get?

"Shalom, I am Bar. I want to perform surgery at your hospital but have no medical license or—what is the word?—training."

"Oh, this is not something you must worry about. Let me find you a scalpel. You can practice on me, if you like."

While it's true that Ms. Refaeli is such a stunner even Jews who aren't her parents think she's an attractive girl, she isn't so exceptional that when she avoided compulsory military service under suspicious circumstances or failed to pay taxes in her home country, Israel was willing to look the other way. In both cases, however, significant compromises were made by Israel that should give Jews everywhere, even those of us outside of our ancestral homeland, a huge case of the Jewish jitters. The military tells a pretty Israeli girl she just has to visit IDF soldiers whenever she's in town and the government lowers her tax rate since she's not predominantly living in the country (both accommodations were made for Ms. Refaeli) and suddenly the weak spot in Israel's armor is revealed. If you want something from the Jewish state, just be unbelievably hot. Problems at a checkpoint? Wear a bikini and you'll walk right through. Want the West Bank? A little makeup and a push-up bra and the land is yours. Worried the Israeli Air Force will bomb your nuclear reactor? Batting a pair of baby blues is as good as any surface-to-air defense missile. We're one lap dance away from losing the whole damn country.

If all that weren't enough, Ms. Refaeli has been romantically involved with Leonardo DiCaprio, on and off again, since 2005. Now, this romance isn't bad for the Jews solely because it makes yentas cry over seeing Ms. Refaeli dating outside the faith. It's bad for us because every time an article or video clip appears online, some idiotic male makes a public comment along the lines of "Hey, Bar, you should dump Leo and settle down with a nice Jewish boy! Call me!" It's pretty embarrassing to read, isn't it? Check any article on the couple, scroll to the comments section, and prepare to cringe.

Fellow Jewish guys, you need to knock it off. Maintain your delusions if you must, but keep them private. It's pretty pathetic when you outdo the stupidity of the anti-Semites making Internet comments above and below yours. Ms. Refaeli is not going to settle down with you just because you're Jewish. Also, she's not going to settle down with you because you're some schmo sitting inside your apartment frittering away on your computer, and she's 2009 *Sports Illustrated* swimsuit cover girl Bar Refaeli. You can't even afford tickets to watch the league she's in.

MARK ZUCKERBERG

Boy-King of Time-Wasting Technology

SO POPULAR! LOOK AT HOW MANY FRIENDS HE HAS

- Cofounded Facebook while still attending Harvard. Some college kids pick up a beer bong, he picked up a computer mouse.
- His site connects hundreds of millions of people, many of whom are not anti-Semites!
- Facebook cosponsored a presidential debate during the 2008 election. His work is of national importance in a very indirect and inconsequential way!
- Ranked as one of *Time*'s most influential people at age twenty-three, and he wasn't even old enough to influence a Hertz employee to let him rent a car.
- The youngest person on the *Forbes* 400 Rich List. Who knew you could make so much money just by letting people talk about themselves?

MORE LIKE FEHBOOK.COM

- Accused of stealing the idea for Facebook from college classmates. Even if the thing you're stealing isn't a tangible thing that anybody needs, a ganef is a ganef, Mr. Zuckerberg.
- Dropped out of Harvard. Your education comes first, young man!

- Site is a serious concern for privacy advocates, who fear it meticulously collects and abuses information about its users. Like that's something our people need to see repeated.
- Willfully allows anti-Israel, anti-Semite, and Holocaust denial groups to operate on Facebook. Worse yet, allows FarmVille updates to inundate news feeds.
- Alters design and amends terms of service so often you need to cut out an hour a day that you would've wasted on Facebook just to review the changes.

By the time he turned twenty-five, Mark Zuckerberg had already amassed a net worth of $4 billion through his social-networking, productivity-slaughtering, soul-crushing online golem, Facebook.com. The urge to smack him in the face with a jealous, angry hand is typical. For those of you who have never heard of Facebook, it is shocking that you are reading this, since you obviously died before 2007. When a Web site boasts 400 million users, not knowing of its existence is the equivalent of not knowing what Brazil is. Mr. Zuckerberg deserves hearty mazel tovs for founding his cyberkingdom, but this boy-pharaoh's success (which is so massive you'd think he invented something that actually helped people) is causing his own people one hell of a headache.

Many Jews might detest Mr. Zuckerberg for allowing his social network to host thousands of interest groups devoted to varying degrees of anti-Semitism—including fan pages with telling spelling like "Fuk All Jews!!!"—but the thing about the site that really causes Jews to plotz comes from creating a profile. The process requires users to label every detail about themselves in the most basic, stark biographical categories: "Birthday," "Sex," "Political Views," "Current City," "Favorite Movies," "Books," "Music," "Education," and "Work," and, of course, "Religious Views." For a Jew, this act of self-description really should be done only under the strict supervision of a psychiatrist. The "Religious Views" field alone ignites an internal soliloquy so epic you'll wish Mr. Zuckerberg had spent his brief college career getting swirlies instead of programming computers.

To type "Jewish" or not to type "Jewish"—that is the question.

The array of "friends" you might have on Facebook often will include barely known associates and acquaintances who might have any number of reactions upon discovering that you're a member of the tribe. Gentile friends who have no problem with Jews but know very few personally may suddenly look to you to satiate their curiosity about the strange Hebrew wanderers they've heard so much about. What are we allowed to eat? Will our eyes bleed if we look upon a cross? And why do so many of us seem to feel especially cold all the time on the crowns of our heads? It's not that setting these people straight would be such a bad or difficult thing, but just because a person is Jewish it doesn't mean they were appointed headmaster at the Mt. Sinai Preparatory School for Goys.

Then there are the associates who we want to have a connection with, but we fear might drop us if they see we're Jewish. The general mantra on who may or may not secretly hate Jews is "you never know." Why risk a perfectly good business or personal relationship just because the person doesn't like Jews—not in a Nazi way, mind you, but a general "Eh, I'd rather not bother with them if I can help it" kind of way. If there were a category for favorite pickle and they listed "candied," would you want to know that information even if it meant you couldn't stand to be in the same room with them because they had such deranged taste in pickles?

Finally, if your passing Facebook acquaintances are Jewish—in like, a very Jewish way—they might think this shared connection entitles them to a level of kinship that you in no way welcome. Every Friday it'll be an invitation on your wall to join them for services and dinner, every Yom Kippur an inquiry as to where you'll be breaking the fast, every Sukkoth a request that you help build a sukkah. Even if you're interested in any of these activities, does the whole world need to know? Oh, but no sooner do you ask this question than you ask yourself another one: *What am I? Am I ashamed of my Judaism? Thank God my zayde is still only on Friendster so he cannot bear witness to the disgrace that is his grandchild!*

In fact, even if you leave "Religious Views" blank, everything else about your profile could have you crashing headlong into a Jewish reckoning. List *The*

Outside Chance of Maximilian Glick as your favorite film, *The Chosen* as your favorite book, and Brandeis as your alma mater, and face the realization that you have no life or interests outside of your religion. List *National Lampoon's Christmas Vacation*, *A Christmas Story*, and Perry Como and discover your unspoken envy of the flock. It's too bad Mr. Zuckerberg didn't invent Twitter. A forum to express yourself to anybody who will listen that doesn't force a person to examine themselves in the process? Now that's a Web site that's good for the Jews.

RAHM EMANUEL

The President's Former Four-and-a-Half-Fingered Right-hand Man

HE KNOWS THE PRESIDENT!

- In high school, he sliced off half of his middle finger while working at an Arby's, but didn't get it treated until it was too late to save it. Not a kvetcher!
- Elected mayor of Chicago in 2011 after representing Illinois' 5th Congressional district from 2003–2009 and serving as White House chief of staff from 2009–2010. Did you not get the e-mails about all of his big job news from his mother?
- Volunteered for civilian service in the IDF during the first Gulf War. He's a fighter! Or, more accurately, a mechanicer!
- Offered a scholarship to the Joffrey Ballet in Chicago. Maybe he even danced with his mother at his bar mitzvah.
- Got a rabbinical waiver to work on the TARP bailout bill through Rosh Hashanah. Not a good excuse for missing services, but at least he cleared it with a rabbi.

NOBODY APPOINTED THIS GUY WHITE HOUSE CHIEF OF BEING BELLIGERENT

- Sat on the board of directors for Freddie Mac and did next to nothing about the fact that the mortgage firm lied about billions in profits. You were on the board of directors. You should've directed them not to do that.

- Has an annoying knuckle-cracking habit and reportedly once cracked his knuckles directly into President Obama's ear. Stop being such a little pisher. The man is the President of the United States of America.
- During a closed-door strategy meeting, allegedly called liberal activists "fucking retarded," which gave Sarah Palin an excuse to talk.
- Before Tony Blair was to meet publicly with President Clinton after the Lewinsky scandal, Mr. Emanuel told the prime minister, "Don't fuck this up." Do you not own a dictionary? Find some new words to use.
- Swears at the most inafuckingppropriate times and places.

The macho tales of President Obama's first Chief of Staff Rahm Emanuel will surely make for a thrilling tell-all one day, but God help the White House intern who dares to write it. If the stories about the fiery politico are at all true, the young man or woman who pens a pulse-pounding account of him will be hunted day and night, night and day, like a pestilent rabbit who threatens a kibbutz's pomegranate orchard. The writer will be given no quarter, for they will have defied "Rahmbo," and Rahmbo shall have his bloody revenge. Kind of makes you think it's not smart to include him in this book. Oh, well.

It's difficult to say with certainty what is fact and what is fiction about Mr. Emanuel. His reputation is shaped by whispers of him sending dead fish to pollsters and stabbing knives into a table while yelling names of his enemies and declaring them "dead!" You know, just the kind of basic psychotic behavior you look for in a man who had unrestricted walk-in privileges to the Oval Office. Regardless of the authenticity of these stories (though the man himself doesn't dispute them), the perception of Mr. Emanuel as a snarling political animal who will eat your face off if you don't see things his way is very real.

In his previous roles as chairs of the Democratic Congressional Campaign Committee and the Democratic Caucus, Mr. Emanuel's Bugsy Siegel–like tenacity fit perfectly. Tasked with finding and fielding Democratic candidates and keeping the left side of the aisle in line, Mr. Emanuel proved a consummate Jewish dad who had no qualms about telling the congressional kids in the backseat to stop fighting and pee in the empty pickle jar, because he would not be stopping the car until they arrived at House Majorityville, USA. But as the de facto administrator of America? Oy, that temper was bound to lead to some problems.

The chief of staff position might as well be called "Secretary of Scapegoating." Only one has ever served for an entire presidential term and when things go bad, they are among the first to be sacrificed—an offering to the masses as an apology for unfulfilled American Dreams. And while the given reason for his departure appears to have more to do with mayoral ambition than absorbing the early failings of his boss, don't count out Mr. Emanuel for taking the hit for those failings just yet. The early exit is standard operating procedure and not to be taken personally, but with this particularly pugnacious and clearly Jewish Jew in the position, there's no way the public, outraged commentary on the man won't carry a tangy zing of anti-Semitism. Of all jobs on Earth, only the Pope seems more ill-suited for us.

Let's hope for a turnaround, but at the time of this writing, Americans are not exactly living in a second Era of Good Feelings. The final verdict on how Mr. Emanuel's abbreviated tenure inside the Obama White House impacted what might come to be known as the Era of Ugh is still unclear, but suffice it to say that a *New York Times Magazine* cover with the headline "The Limits of Rahmism: He Was Chosen as White House Chief of Staff Because He Could Make Things Happen. What Happened?" will not be tacked up on any temple bulletin boards. Around the second anniversary of President Obama's election, Richard Wolffe's *Revival: The Struggle for Survival Inside the Obama White House* offered a glimpse into the future of the blame game, writing, "[O]ther senior staffers believed that Emanuel's excess energy was a major part of the problem . . . 'It's all tactics and no strategy,' said one of Emanuel's close colleagues. . . . 'And his style is unbelievably bad. It's just too abusive.' " Now, that might not scream 'we're all in this mess because of the Jew,' but it also doesn't scream 'we'd love to have you back if running the City of Chicago doesn't pan out, Rahm!' And while "excess energy" and "unbelievably bad [style]" may not make the cut as far as anti-Semitic coded language goes, doesn't it kind of sound like these unnamed staffers are just describing your argumentative cousin who's into politics? It's alright if you're too afraid to answer. After all, you never know if Rahmbo is standing right behind you.

PHILIP ROTH

Please, Tell Us More About Your Penis

NO WONDER YOU LIKE WRITING ABOUT YOURSELF

- Winner of over 20 literary awards, including the Pulitzer Prize. Now, Mr. Roth, you did thank your parents when accepting every one of them, correct?
- Served in the United States Army. So well-rounded to be good with the pen *and* the sword.
- Street in New Jersey where he grew up renamed in his honor. God willing, it's not one of those vile penis-shaped cul-de-sacs.
- Taught at the University of Chicago, the University of Iowa, Princeton University, and the University of Pennsylvania. You should see if he would write a letter of recommendation for your son Benjamin's college application.
- One of the most celebrated authors of the modern era, and he became so without having to write ridiculous stories about secret societies who don't want anybody to know Jesus had a kid.

PORTNOY ISN'T THE ONLY ONE WHO HAS SOME COMPLAINTS

- Looking to make your mother hate you? Tell her she reminds you of a female character in a Philip Roth novel.

- According to ex-wife Claire Bloom's memoir, not the nicest husband. See above.
- Focuses all his talent and energy on airing our tsuris to the world at large.
- A giant depressing noodge who believes the novel will be extinct in a quarter century.
- Fairly egotistical to make yourself the centerpiece of most of your work, don't you think?

What do you say in a book about Jews to the writer who has been the definitive chronicler of the Jewish-American postwar experience? Shut up. That's what. Sheket, sheket, sheket. A lot of Jewish community outrage is directed at Philip Roth because of his supposed uncomplimentary presentation of our culture. Detractors take issue with his guilt-ridden, neurotic, perverted characterizations, particularly in works like *Portnoy's Complaint* and the short stories in *Goodbye, Columbus*. This portrayal is three things: vulgar, embarrassing, and, above all, highly accurate. He's not self-hating, he's self-aware. What critics should take issue with is the fact that this brilliant storyteller has chosen to use his gifts to let every literate Gentile in the world know what it's like to be a Jew in America. They don't need to know, Mr. Roth!

Most of us spend our whole lives burying our Jewish-American experiences and thoughts, trying not to let the outside, larger society know what an unbearable tokhes-ache it is to get along as a Jew. Then this writer comes along with stories like "Eli, The Fanatic," "Defender of the Faith," the Zuckerman novels, and *Operation Shylock,* and kvetches his head off—for all to read—about the struggle secular Jews have dealing with our more Orthodox brethren, Gentiles, and ourselves. Who needs to know such things? Over the course of time, we've become relatively good at gulping down our fears and grievances. We're just trying to be civil, trying not to make a fuss. Do we not know our place in this world? Do we mentally potch ourselves trying to reconcile our Judaism with our Americanism? Do we have a massive victim complex? Absolutely. That's what happens when the majority of a people's history is predicated on other people trying to exterminate them. But that doesn't mean we want to bother everybody with our constant internal tsuris. That's what our family and Jewish friends are for.

The old adage is "write what you know," but doesn't Philip Roth know anything else? How about some nice stories about casual solid two-button collared shirts? There must be a great novel about having luscious eyebrows just waiting to be written. Honestly, any other narrative besides one revolving around the deepest, most uncomfortable aspects of our existence would be preferred.

Now, about the shmekl. It's terrific that Mr. Roth has a creative outlet to articulate his every unique predilection and method employed during the course of masturbation. What would be helpful to us, however, is if he could—rather than indelibly linking such activities to the Jewish-American character—write his opuses on wanking in an entirely separate story that has nothing to do with Jews. Then, for good measure, light that story on fire. Whatever Mr. Roth's intentions, be they to represent in graphic detail the clash between Jewish propriety and American hedonism or to shatter disgustingly the myth of the tiny Hebraic penis, he could have had the decency to minimize the audacity of the self-gratification. Certainly any central figure in a Roth novel would understand the discomfort felt when goyim meet you for the first time and immediately speculate over how many times and in what unorthodox locations you've jerked it since lunch.

Finally, as if reveling in Jewish-American strains, trials, and foibles weren't enough, Mr. Roth has of late become something of a Semitic Stephen King, replacing Cujo with the Third Reich. If you've ever had one of those lazy, lemonade-in-hand days where you sit in the sun and casually contemplate, "I wonder what the Holocaust would be like if it were even more horrifying," Mr. Roth has attempted to satisfy your curiosity with *The Plot Against America*, in which Nazism spreads to the States. It's as if he was afraid he wasn't giving Jews enough to stress about and thought he'd present us with a new nightmare to mull over. We get it, Mr. Roth. Being Jewish is often hard and occasionally scary. Now can you please stop telling everybody that?

JILL ZARIN

Real Housewife of Every Jew's Nightmares

IN REALITY, SHE IS PROBABLY A WONDERFUL JEWISH MOTHER

- Named one of the 25 Most Stylish New Yorkers in *US Weekly.* Giant bracelets must be in!
- Became a spokesperson for Kodak. Oh, good. We were worried Jewish mothers would forget to photographically document every second of their children's lives.
- Actively involved in many charities for arthritis research, Kenyan schoolhouses, and the developmentally disabled. A woman of many mitzvoth, even if they are all documented by reality-show cameras.
- Writes books with her mother and sister, and manages a business with her husband. Stays close with mishpocha even while she works!
- Looks like she's very good at putting on her own eye makeup.

IN REALITY TELEVISION, WHO KNOWS WHAT SHE IS

- Puts her family on camera for all the world to see. This is good parenting? Do you know what kind of deranged people could be watching?
- Gets into heated, dramatic conflicts with her costars about matters normally left behind in grade school. Stop acting like such a spoiled vilde chaya—especially while everybody is watching you on television.

- Complains about problems most people would kill to have. You should be so lucky!
- Bragged about selling her Hamptons home before the market collapsed. A little gauche, Jill, a little gauche.
- Just because you're good at putting on eye makeup, it doesn't mean you have to use the world's total supply of it everyday. Save some for the rest of civilization!

Unlike her Bravo reality TV compatriot Patti Stanger, Jill Zarin of *The Real Housewives of New York City* is on camera for no reason at all. She's not helping people find love, providing useful services, or displaying any discernible talent. She, along with her East Coast coven of well-to-duhs, seems to be a walking twenty-first-century Cartesian maxim: she appears on television, therefore she has a show. The life of Mrs. Zarin looks like it's all apples and honey, replete with trips to the Hamptons, dinner parties galore, and intensive apartment redecorating projects. The personal flare-ups between herself and the other fancy-schmancy women who are inexplicably called "housewives" generally take place on tennis courts, at charity events, or during soirees sponsored by magazines. In other words, this isn't exactly a penetrating look at the hardships of life in the shtetl.

Mrs. Zarin isn't any better or worse than anybody else in the ensemble (though each woman appears to judge herself the best and most sane of the bunch) and watching the videotaped toils of the upper crust provides many people a guilty viewing pleasure. Strictly in her role on the show, Mrs. Zarin is not bad for the Jews. Every unwarranted hissy fit, every disingenuous proclamation that she wants to clear the air or apologize, every clawing attempt to reclaim her youthful appearance is matched by all the other housewives, regardless of religion. Hair color is pretty much the most notable and defining marker in figuring out which one is which, although the one who insists on being called a countess helps with the identification process.

Also like all of the other dubiously real ladies, Mrs. Zarin has parlayed her newly recognizable name into nontelevised revenue streams, but her specific endeavor does our people no good whatsoever. While the other Madam New Yorkers were content to put out farkakte etiquette guides or diet margaritas or jewelry lines or their boobs in *Playboy,* Mrs. Zarin went the way of the advice book and released *Secrets of a Jewish Mother: Real Advice, Real Stories, Real Love.*

Secrets. Of. A. Jewish. Mother.

That is an actual title of a real hardcover book that anybody with $25.95 or a library card can read. If you were to purchase it from Amazon or BarnesAndNoble.com, it could even come gift wrapped. What kind of a sick world do we live in where that kind of information can be disseminated openly to any person who wants it? We have laws against sharing national security information with foreign enemies, but this is considered OK? Would you like to save some money and know what the big secret to being a Jewish mother is? Well tough tokhes. You're not going to find out here or anywhere else. Nobody outside of God himself can articulate, let alone teach, whatever it is that goes on inside the head of a Jewish mother. It's like trying to imagine the infinitude of the universe. Think about it for too long and you'll soon find yourself gripping your brow in agony.

The truly unbelievable aspect to Mrs. Zarin's book is the brazen claims in its promotion. On the book's Web site, a blog post posits: "Despite what you may think, you do not need to be Jewish to be a Jewish mother. Nor do you need to be a parent. Being a Jewish mother means carrying yourself with a certain attitude that is not necessarily confrontational, but always assertive." Wrong! Damnable lies! To be a Jewish mother, one has to be both Jewish and a mother. The components that make up the person are right in the description. It's as if Mrs. Zarin were to hand you a recipe for cherry pie that included neither cherries nor piecrust. The statement is just so fundamentally false that it's bound to trigger animosity in anybody who puts their time and money into the book. And that's not even mentioning the tome's glaring contradiction that makes one question its veracity and authenticity entirely. It is supposedly written by the all-Jewish trio of Mrs. Zarin; her mother, Gloria Kamen; and her sister, Lisa Wexler, but how in the world would any Jewish mother, let alone three, have time to write a book in between phone calls to her children? Then again, maybe that's another Jewish mother secret we'll never understand.

BADDEST FOR THE JEWS

AMY WINEHOUSE

Soulful Singer Who Very Likely Doesn't Know Where She Is Right Now

SHE COULD'VE BEEN SUCH A LOVELY CANTOR

- In less than 7 years has amassed 23 awards, including 5 Grammys. She probably even accepted a few of them while fully conscious.
- Cowrites her own music, unlike those Gentile pop princesses.
- Claims to attend shul on Yom Kippur. It's something!
- Has said she has the musical taste of "an old Jewish man," which of course means she has exceptional taste.
- Pled guilty to assault charges. OK, not great, but at least she admitted what she did was wrong.

WHO CAN SEE THAT PRETTY PUNIM UNDER ALL THAT MAKEUP?

- Due to intoxication or exhaustion, regularly cancels or cuts short her performances—performances that people have paid to see, young lady!
- Unable to complete the theme for a James Bond movie because of who knows what kind of problem. What's so difficult, Amy? You go in, you sing the song, you go home.
- Screamed obscenities while sitting in the audience of a children's theatre performance. Save the cursing for when you have your own children.

- The tattoos, the implants, the smoking, the booze, the drugs. Are you trying to set a world record for desecrations to a body?
- Just a question, Amy: When is the last time you took a shower?

There's something to be said for a female entertainer who refuses to fall into the cliché of the good Jewish girl. That something, however, is not that it's wise to go completely off the deep end while doing it. The only way Amy Winehouse could be more of a mess is if she . . . actually, there is no way she could be more of a mess. Once you hit tattoo number twelve, converse with a baby mouse and sing a racist song (that includes a string of anti-Semitic slurs, among others) on YouTube, have multiple run-ins with the law, receive two years probation for assaulting a theatre manager during a children's performance of *Cinderella,* drink yourself into oblivion, take up a mild plastic surgery addiction, get married to an abusive shegetz who turns you on to hard drugs, and proceed to do those hard drugs along with every other drug on the planet, there's pretty much no more mess to be made.

Oy, Ms. Winehouse! What happened? We're Jews, for God's sake. We're not supposed to have drug-addled meltdowns. We're not cool enough for that kind of thing. That's for Jim Morrison, Janis Joplin, and Jimi Hendrix—artists who never had the inborn, crippling fear of their parents catching them under the influence of anything other than Manischewitz and forever feeling the sting of unyielding disappointment. We develop late-in-life addictions to ibuprofen and Lipitor, not crack cocaine.

Sadly, scolding the singer here won't do any good, and not just because she probably has lost so many brain cells that she no longer possesses the cognitive ability to read. She has progressed (or would it be regressed?) to the point where, despite her feeling that "at the end of the day, I'm a Jewish girl," most of the public thinks of her first and foremost as a time-traveling zombie songbird beamed here from the early 1960s. The travesty is the trademark.

A separation between the artist and the art might have alleviated the situation. Ideally, hearing your Jewish daughter singing a song off of *Back To Black* shouldn't immediately set off visions of a sheyne meydel with your DNA falling facedown on the sidewalk while paparazzi encircle her. When Ms. Winehouse's worldwide hit is called "Rehab" and its overarching message is an aversion to it, however, such a separation is impossible. You'll be driving her to school and she'll be in the backseat crooning sweetly about the joys of substance abuse. Not a great way to start your morning.

Ms. Winehouse's downward spiral is so hard to swallow because, damn it, we just thought one of our people wouldn't fall into the same pop-culture tiger trap as a Britney Spears or a Lindsay Lohan. The hope that somehow our overwrought compulsion to succeed would block out the social and chemical poisons that often befall those who enjoy a meteoric rise appears to be false. It's not like we're asking her to fulfill some grand notion of Jewish superiority. Nobody's asking her to win a MacArthur genius grant, mind you. It'd be nice, though, to feel secure in thinking that any talented young Jewish woman who becomes a pop sensation would be smart enough to avoid getting into bar fights, stumbling into lampposts, marrying lowlife scum, and overall, looking like a train wreck that has crashed into another train wreck.

JACK ABRAMOFF

Purchaser of Fine Legislation Since 1994

A JEW WITH A SOLID, STURDY FRAME

- Decided to become a Baal teshuva Jew at age 12. A self-motived Jew in addition to being a self-motivated criminal.
- Was supposedly physically fit at one point. He weight lifted in high school. So that's nice for him.
- Earned a JD from Georgetown University, presumably so he could learn all the laws he would eventually break.
- Appointed by President Reagan to the United States Holocaust Memorial Council. Maybe he managed not to do anything illegal in that capacity?
- Wrote and produced his own movie that only lost several million dollars.
- Founded the Eshkol Academy for Jewish boys, which was made possible by the generous contributions of Mr. Abramoff's clients. More on those contributions later . . .

IF YOU'RE SUCH A GOOD LOBBYIST, HOW IS IT THAT YOU CAN'T CONVINCE ANYBODY YOU'RE NOT A TOTAL BASTARD?

- Bribed and influenced politicians with you name it: Extravagant trips, payoffs, event tickets, fancy meals. You couldn't have just presented an informed argument, Jack?
- Lobbied for the Commonwealth of the Northern Mariana Islands and helped it maintain federal labor exemptions while covering up its alleged sex-slave trade. Were you taking part in a moral repugnance contest or something?
- Offered to help the government of Sudan with the image problems a regime typically garners after carrying out genocide. Jack does not appear to be a student of his own people's history.
- Served almost six years in prison for fraud, conspiracy, and tax evasion . . . and that's *after* cooperating with authorities.
- About that Jewish school he founded. Turns out his clients didn't know they were generously contributing to it.

To the outsider, lobbying is a curious profession. One of those occupations like "professional blogger" and "concert promoter" that makes you scratch your head and ask, "That's an actual job? You can make money doing that?" Lobbying seems to involve eating lots of nice dinners, having conversations with lawmakers, and giving lovely gifts as a thank-you to those lawmakers for taking the time to have the aforementioned conversations. Simply put, it's schmoozing, and since Jews invented the term, it stands to reason that we'd be pretty good at it. Maybe then it should come as no surprise that one of the most prominent pro schmoozers was Baal teshuva Jew and former Federal Correctional Institution, Cumberland inmate, Jack Abramoff. Why did Mr. Abramoff serve time? Well, as it turns out, Mr. Abramoff completely sucked at trying to influence politicians through the use of ideas and reason, so instead he just bought them a whole bunch of crap that dazzled them into passing or preventing legislation, depending on the needs of his clients.

It does seem a little unfair to castigate Mr. Abramoff for supposedly living by a strict religious code that was often at direct odds with his professional conduct. The laws of Orthodox Judaism are nothing if not complex, so maybe he just got confused while studying the Mishnah. He has the tact of a gorilla; perhaps he has the reading comprehension skills of one as well. Besides, the purpose of this endeavor is not to determine whether he is a bad Jew, but rather to explain why he is bad for the Jews. On that front, there is nothing complex about Mr. Abramoff's transgressions.

Given that he used millions of dirty dollars in order to surreptitiously wield influence over the government, there aren't many more racist stereotypes Mr. Abramoff could have on his resume that could give the Jew-haters' tongues something to wag about. He'd have to go well outside of his purview as a lobbyist and do something crazy like use the Hollywood system to make a thinly veiled propaganda film. Oh, wait, he did that when he wrote and produced 1989's *Red Scorpion,* starring Dolph Lundgren as a Soviet killer who goes to Africa and realizes his commie bosses are the real bad guys. It would have been a great message movie if not for two things: First, the phrase "starring Dolph Lundgren" doesn't quite carry the gravitas needed to spur societal change. Second, according to *Harper's Magazine,* Mr. Abramoff's film was secretly funded by the apartheid government of South Africa, who were, as you might recall, megaracists. So in one fell swoop Mr. Abramoff used Hollywood in an attempt to manipulate audiences and displayed unbridled greed in his willingness to take money from anybody, no matter how morally repugnant they are. If he was so intent on fulfilling some of the most vile clichés about Jews, the least he could have done was write a halfway watchable movie. And good God . . . Dolph Lundgren?

Part of what got Mr. Abramoff into his biggest heap of trouble—the heap that landed him in the big concrete building where everybody has a nickname and nobody wants to know how it was earned—was his double-dealings while lobbying for Native American interests. Apparently, in the lobbying trade, it's bad form to bilk $85 million out of your client, use that money to secretly lobby against them in order to increase the necessity (and fees) for your services, and then illegally act on their behalf by bribing elected and appointed officials. You'd think that being part of a similarly minuscule ethnic group would inspire Mr. Abramoff to help, not dupe, the tribes, but it appears his top allegiance was to a small group of green-faced dead presidents.

Here's the part that really screws the Jews though. Mr. Abramoff wasn't content to be just another DC-based greedy bastard; he had to enrich Jewish causes with the millions he swindled. He simply took the money the Native Americans gave him and dropped it into his Judaic pet causes. That's right, the schmuck had to drag us all unknowingly into his mishegoss. Funds from the tribes went to Jewish settlers in the West Bank and the establishment of an Orthodox Jewish preparatory school in Maryland. No matter how you feel about the causes, it's hard to imagine they are high priorities on the Choctaw agenda.

The shyster wasn't even content to keep his loathsome dealings restricted to finances. He had to refer to his Native American clients as a bunch of "monkeys" and "troglodytes," just to add some racist icing to his criminal cake. So, thanks to his resoundingly putzy efforts, we now have a whole new group of people hating us for a completely justified reason.

Any other groups whose ire you'd like directed at us, Mr. Abramoff? There might be some Jains in India who don't have anything against us yet. Or how about the Maori in New Zealand? They seem like nice people who could hate the Jews if you gave them a good enough reason. Or maybe you want to branch out into nonhuman groups? Hundreds of bear cubs are out there just waiting to be stolen, and their protective mothers would certainly make the most formidable anti-Semites since the Spanish inquisitors. Really, Mr. Abramoff. If you're going to be a such a schmuck, at least have the decency not to set the bar so low for yourself.

ALAN GREENSPAN

Anybody Understand What This Guy Is Talking About?

CHAIRMENSCH OF THE FEDERAL RESERVE

- A Juilliard-trained musician. The realization that he'd never earn any money as a clarinetist was perhaps the greatest economic forecast he ever made in his life.
- Ph.D. in economics from NYU, so at least he had the academic credentials to back up all of his blunders.
- Served for both Republican and Democrat presidents as Chairman of the Federal Reserve from 1987–2006. Everybody likes him!
- Successfully managed a stock-market crash only two months after he started on the job. Even though he never made it as a musician, he still became a one-hit wonder.
- Awarded a Presidential Medal of Freedom, a Department of Defense Medal for Distinguished Public Service, a Dwight D. Eisenhower Medal for Leadership and Service, a Thomas Jefferson Foundation Medal in Citizen Leadership, a Harry S. Truman Medal for Economic Policy, and the titles of both Knight Commander of the British Empire and Commander of the *Légion d'honneur*. And just think how many awards he would have won if more people could figure out what he did for a living.

HERE ARE A FEW REASONS WHY YOU'RE BROKE

- Cut interest rates so low that people collected mortgages like baseball cards.
- In 2004, claimed that adjustable-rate mortgages were a good deal and then eight days later, when nobody was listening because they were all out getting ARMs, stated that fixed-rate mortgages might not be so bad after all.
- Criticized by both Republicans and Democrats throughout tenure as chairman. Nobody likes him!
- Admitted in 2008 that he "made a mistake in presuming that the self-interests of organizations, specifically banks and others, were such that they were best capable of protecting their own shareholders and their equity in the firms." Yeah, that was kind of a big mistake.
- Disciple of Ayn Rand and her Objectivist philosophy of self-interest, which is an ongepotchket way of saying "greedy."

Former Chairman of the Federal Reserve Alan Greenspan has a gift for language, and like so many Hanukkah presents from elderly Jews, his gift generally leaves people disappointed and confused. The man who charted America's—and, to a large extent, the world's—monetary destiny for nineteen years successfully handled what could have been an all-out economic meltdown following the 1987 crash, but he is also one of the biggest blameworthy figures in the financial crisis of the twenty-first century's first decade. He also is fond of mentioning that he read financial reports and wrote his memoirs while soaking in a bathtub, which is an image nobody ever asked him to describe.

What is about to be said is not very nice and it's probably not very smart, but try if you can to read all the way through with an open mind. Dr. Greenspan's Jewishness—his yiddishkeyt—is part of the reason he got us into this mess (just a part, not the whole reason. Please don't be mad!). Now there was nothing intentionally nefarious about his actions and any Jew-haters celebrating this admission should still feel free to go shtup themselves, but the fact is, Dr. Greenspan spoke to the nation in an abstract, obscure, and altogether indecipherable manner that approached a near Talmudic level of complexity. It's how our rabbis and grandfathers have spoken for thousands of years. None of us ever understand what the hell they're talking about, and it's fair to assume that sometimes they don't even know what the hell they're talking about, but nevertheless we let them prattle on with their spiel because it's not worth getting yelled at for interrupting them. Instead of actually listening to what these wise men have to say, which would result in God knows what kind of headache, we've learned to simply tune them out. It might be a little disrespectful, but it helps make life the only thing Jews want it to be: tolerable.

Unfortunately, while Jews are very well acquainted with Dr. Greenspan's cryptic, aged patois and know that it's best to just ignore it, most of the world is not. This very understandable unfamiliarity led to much of the ruin. It would be terrific if Jews understood Dr. Greenspan and could use that comprehension to our financial advantage, but the language of the zayde is one that sounds like garble even to members of his own tribe. Indeed, the man himself admitted once, "I guess I should warn you, if I turn out to be particularly clear, you've probably misunderstood what I've said." But Dr. Greenspan was the chairman of the Federal Reserve, so every time he opened his mouth and said things like "How do we know when irrational exuberance has unduly escalated asset values?", everybody would lose their minds trying to interpret and parse his enigmatic jabber, rather than responding, as any good Jewish grandchild would, with a placating nod.

The market swung, often wildly, following one of these oracular proclamations. Instead of behaving like normal congregants who, during a service, are more focused on what they might want to eat at the Oneg Shabbat than about what their rabbi is saying, the world's market watchers listened too closely to Dr. Greenspan's sermons. Financial analysts were unaware that old Jewish men just enjoy pulling people aside and talking about what interests them. Sometimes they don't even bother conversing with anybody in particular, choosing instead to sit in the most comfortable chair in living room and talk over everybody else's conversation until Passover seder is ready at the table. Usually their favorite topics are the history of the Jewish farmer, or the history of the Jewish athlete, or the history of the Jewish violinist, but Dr. Greenspan apparently liked talking numbers. And, oh, did he have a captive audience. The man could break wind at a congressional hearing and the next day the economy of a small Asian country would collapse. On his best day, a senior rabbi couldn't command such attention.

None of this is to say that Dr. Greenspan, or any Jew for that matter, shouldn't be chairman of the Federal Reserve. The Greenspan Mystique wasn't the sole cause of the world's monetary troubles, and not everything he said caused a further flushing of the financial toilet. Maybe, though, future elderly Jewish chairmen (Benjamin Benanke, you're not getting any younger) should take precautions against becoming too mystifying in their remarks. In fact, why not take a page from rabbis and have a cantor by your side to break up your economic forecasts with some soothing musical interludes? If the Kol Nidre teaches us anything, it is that sometimes, in the course of reflecting on the past and trying to act wiser in the coming year, a little singing can aid in one's clarity. Maybe then people will do the smart thing by dismissing the Chairman's advice and choosing instead to actually look at their own bank account before deciding whether or not they can afford to buy a house.

DOV CHARNEY

Clothier . . . or Pornographer. Kind of Tough to Tell.

HE RUNS HIS OWN BUSINESS, YOU KNOW

- Self-made entrepreneur who started his business out of a college dorm room. That's no easy thing. Have you seen how tiny those rooms are?
- Proudly makes all his clothes in America. No dreck material here. Why, you could pass these T-shirts on to your children!
- Employs a largely immigrant core of workers and pays them double the minimum wage plus benefits. Not only does he make clothes, he makes mitzvoth!
- Number 19 on the 2009 Finalist list of *Time*'s 100. Who knew selling monochromatic T-shirts could make a man so important?
- Passionate promoter of immigration reform, and do you where any American Jews would be without immigration? Well, not in America, obviously.

WHY NOT TRY PUTTING ALL THOSE NICE CLOTHES YOU MAKE ON YOUR NAKED MODELS

- Hit with numerous sexual harassment lawsuits and, according to Gawker.com, makes employees sign a confidentiality agreement that carries a $1 million penalty for whistle-blowing. It's surprising such a savvy businessman didn't realize he could dramatically decrease legal costs by not sexually harassing workers.

- Once engaged in oral sex with an employee and masturbated while a reporter was interviewing him for an article. Is this how you try to impress people?
- Over 1,500 employees found to be working illegally. It's nice you're giving people jobs, but you should make an effort to keep it kosher, Dov.
- Used an image of Woody Allen dressed as a rabbi in a billboard without the man's permission. How would you like it if somebody used an artistic representation of your image without permission? Say for instance, in this book?
- Often uses topless models who look like they could be in middle school. You're in your early forties! Save the dirty alter kocker shtick for later.

Not being the most classically handsome of men, despite the protestations of our mothers, many Jewish males put all their energy into being attractive in other, less aesthetic ways. We'll be funny, we'll work hard, we'll spread the rumor that, while you'd never guess it by looking at us, we're surprisingly talented in bed (by the way, nobody buys that one), or we'll just hope for the fail-safe option shared by every homely male schlemiel of a small religious subset: find a pretty girl who only wants to be with a man of the same faith. Many a lapsed Jew has suddenly found HaShem when faced with a beautiful head of curls. And then there is Dov Charney, who has circumvented all the hard work Jewish men have to do in order to get close to the beautiful folk by founding a goddamn T-shirt company.

For the unacquainted, Mr. Charney is the CEO of American Apparel, which is the largest clothing manufacturer that operates in the United States. If you've ever walked down a metropolitan sidewalk and seen a scruffy-cheeked twenty-something male or a lanky, disheveled female, and he or she was texting on a six-hundred-dollar phone despite the unlikelihood that they have a job, chances are that they are wearing a creation of Mr. Charney's.

Much like his throwback look of fitted, simple clothing, Mr. Charney is a retro-style Jew—a self-described "Jewish hustler"—who entered the shmatte trade like the rag merchants of a bygone era, before most American Jews traded in their needle and thread for a corporate key card and chance to yell at overprivileged Ivy League underlings. Unlike his mercantile ancestors, however, Mr. Charney uses a complex modern marketing technique known informally as "Hey, look! Boobs!" It's hard to tell if his company's Web site is meant to sell clothes or serve as a soft-core porn page for people who want to fool themselves into thinking they're clicking on it for reasons other than to look at scantily clad women. *Playboy* has its articles, AmericanApparel.net has its satin charmeuse jumper pant.

Anybody who has ever walked by an Abercrombie & Fitch store and seen the window displays of bare-chested, wind-tussled goyim wearing breathable chinos knows the overt use of sexuality in apparel advertising is nothing new. Mr. Charney shouldn't be demonized for tying his products to sex because it is, after all, the thing that sells. In fact, he should be applauded for bucking the trend of airbrushing and photoshopping by featuring so-called real women in his campaigns. It'd just be nice if he put some distance between himself and the models—at the very least a distance longer than his penis.

Oh, that's right, he often personally photographs his models in his office or homes shortly before or after shtupping them. Sometimes you can even see his pantless legs or half of his hirsute face in American Apparel advertisements, which is quite an ingenious way to violently shift the eye's focus to anything in the picture that is not him. Mr. Charney doesn't try to hide the fact that he carries on sexual relationships with his employees, and even makes new workers sign forms acknowledging that American Apparel is a sexually charged work environment. This is like cows signing a document acknowledging that there are a lot of sharp objects in a slaughterhouse. It doesn't necessarily mean they're going to end up as a T-bone, but there's definitely a better-than-average chance. Unsurprisingly, he's been hit by a litany of sexual harassment lawsuits and earned a reputation as a first-rate pervert. As entrepreneurial and well-intentioned as he might be, a central tenant of Mr. Charney's company seems to be Get The Boss Laid, and when a Jewish boss fashions himself less like Yves Saint Laurent and more like a lecher trolling for trollops, people tend to think that reflects poorly on his people.

MONICA LEWINSKY

Inappropriately Special Assistant to President Clinton

SHE MADE QUITE AN IMPRESSION ON THE PRESIDENT

- Began as an unpaid intern but was promoted to a paid position in the White House Office of Legislative Affairs, quite possibly for merit-based, nonsexual reasons.
- Won immunity from the Office of the Independent Counsel without having to plead guilty. Oy, thank God. Finding a husband was going to be hard enough for her without having a criminal record.
- Appeared on *Saturday Night Live* following her scandal. From scandal to shtick in just a few short months!
- Served as a U.S. trend reporter for Britain's Channel 5. Apparently the hot trend that year was putting Monica Lewinsky on television for no good reason.
- Holds a masters in social psychology from the London School of Economics. Something on her resume that didn't result from notoriety caused by oral sex!

AND THE PRESIDENT MADE QUITE AN IMPRESSION ON HER . . . DRESS

- Had sexual encounters with the president in his private study, the Oval Office, and the bathroom by the Oval Office. So enjoy thinking about that on your White House tour.

- According to the *Washington Post,* didn't have a "substantive conversation" with the president until two and a half months into their affair. But, Monica, how would you know if he'd make a good father for your future children?
- Used her name recognition to make a bunch of chazarai handbags and shill for weight-loss centers. Would simply laying low really have been so difficult?
- All that schmoozing in fancy Manhattan social circles after the investigation? The road to redemption doesn't start with a bunch of yentas gossiping about you in Page Six.
- Demanded President Clinton help secure her a job following their affair. Congratulations, Monica. You've discovered the one way a Jewish parent wouldn't be proud of their child's career advancement.

What's that? Monica Lewinsky should be left alone? It's been well over a decade since the scandal that rocked and titillated the world and we've all moved on? OK, you're right. Hope your zaftig Jewish daughter's application to be a White House intern goes well. After all, staffers who are singularly focused on helping the President of the United States of America not embarrass himself would have no subconscious wariness about hiring a young woman who shares superficial traits with a person who participated in an affair that ultimately resulted in the second impeachment in history. Also, if your daughter did snag the job, surely there would be no snickering that went on behind her back. Comments like, "Whoa, don't leave that one alone with the president," "Who let in the Lewinsky," and "Let's hope she's gets her dresses dry-cleaned promptly" would never be uttered by coworkers, let alone the fair-minded punditry who always choose to keep their sound bites limited to facts and not idiotic comparisons made solely for the sake of garnering attention. Yes, yes, Ms. Lewinsky's oral activities are in the past and presidential sex scandals only capture the imagination of the public insofar as their resulting legal consequences.

Now, back to the real world.

Unfortunately, in a class of fleeting 1990s newsmakers, Ms. Lewinsky is a standout. We're not talking about some unscrupulous figure skater's husband taking a nightstick to the competition's knees, or an abusive goy getting his phallus chopped off at the hands of his apoplectic wife. We're talking about a young woman whose acts of fellatio, which she performed on the leader of the free world, were meticulously documented in a congressional report. This is not the kind of overachieving we like to see in our Jewish youth. President Clinton was no doubt complicit (if not mostly responsible) for the tawdry business, and certainly Ms. Lewinsky cannot be blamed for the president perjuring himself, but what a letdown for the Jews. The young and ambitious Jews among us are no better than anybody else and they make mistakes. On the other hand, it'd be nice to believe that Jews have enough respect for decorum that if we were standing in a room with the president and a cigar, his hands would be by his sides and the cigar would be in a mouth. It's a simple dream for our people, but a good one.

What made the Lewinsky scandal (as it is now formally titled as if Horndog Clinton wasn't even involved in the matter) surpass an unfortunate youthful mistake for the eponymous intern, however, were the subsequent moves to capitalize on the whole megillah. The book, the handbags, the commercials for Jenny Craig, the hosting of a reality dating show called *Mr. Personality*—in which a woman tries to select a husband from a group of twenty bachelors who, by the way, are all wearing spooky gladiatoresque masks the whole time—these are not the pursuits of a person trying to return to a normal life. Ms. Lewinsky often cited her exorbitant legal bills resulting from the scandal as the reason she took on such work, which often paid her six to seven figures. As understandable as that might be, it's hard to suppress the gut retort, "Well, then, maybe you shouldn't go down on married presidents! Good God, it was the White House! People are trying to get work done there!" Let's put it this way: If your first acting credit on IMDb is "*Bill Clinton Testimony Tapes* (1998) (V) . . . Herself," stop there! No matter the real reasons for keeping yourself in the spotlight, at the end of the day it looks like you're trying to earn a buck off of a blowjob, and that perception is not something any Jewish person should be upholding.

Ms. Lewinsky has said she was in love with President Clinton and, hey, sometimes the heart wants what the heart wants, logic and reason and eternal shame be damned. It's just unfortunate she had to feel this way while serving in a capacity that many ambitious young Jews hope to find themselves. No, not that "capacity." Don't be so vulgar! The Washington intern capacity. No Jewish parent wants to put the brakes on their child's political dreams, but now the fear that your kid could go to Washington and end up in the center of a national scandal is real. Acceptance into the White House intern program should be cause for a celebration, not an awkward preemptive discussion about why performing sex acts on the president will cause your mameleh to die from dehydration after she cries out all of her bodily fluids. In Ms. Lewinsky, Jews saw their daughters and sisters, and, thanks to the lustful nature of the transgressions, felt totally gross about having the vision. When you think about your child in the corridors of power, you're not envisioning them on their knees.

ELIOT SPITZER

Lover of Justice and Shiksas Who Let You Do Them for Money

A DEFENDER OF THE COMMON MAN

- A BA from Princeton and a JD from Harvard. You'd think with all that education he'd be smart enough not to get caught visiting prostitutes.
- Dismantled the Gambino crime family while in the Manhattan DA's office. Congratulations on somehow not ending up in an airtight barrel at the bottom of the Hudson for that one.
- Became New York State Attorney General and rooted out white-collar corruption, although maybe he should've focused more on his personal lipstick-on-the-collar corruption.
- Overwhelmingly elected governor of New York. Also overwhelmingly asked to resign.
- Managed to get his own show on CNN after his downfall. It took a lot of chutzpah to reenter the public eye after what he went through. Or maybe shamelessness. OK, 10 percent chutzpah, 90 percent shamelessness.

A PATRONIZER OF THE "PROFESSIONAL" WOMAN

- As governor, ordered New York State Police to spy on his political rivals. People could be driving like maniacs down the Taconic and he's pulling cops off the street to stare at his enemies through peepholes?
- Blamed and suspended aides in wake of his ethics scandal. Take responsibility for your own mistakes, Eliot.
- The thing with the hookers. A shande!
- Used campaign funds to pay for the hotel where he did the shtupping. Pay for your putz on your own dime, governor.
- Dragged his poor wife out to stand behind him while he admitted guilt.

Eliot Spitzer had so many things going for him. A young, smart, ambitious lawyer with the heart of a mensch and the ferocity of a Maccabean warrior. Sure, the hairline was a little untidy and his beady eyes made him look like a serpent with a penchant for frotteurism, but on the whole, the governor seemed like he just might be the next great hope for the first Jewish president. Imagine! A United States president who was not just a Jew, but a fairly physically fit Jew. For his tough stance on crime as New York's Attorney General, he earned the nickname "Eliot Ness" and, as every Jew knows, when a nickname is bestowed upon you by the masses and there is nothing even remotely anti-Semitic about it, it is likely the highest level of acceptance you will ever achieve.

When Mr. Spitzer's own attorney general, Andrew Cuomo, started investigating the governor's improper use of state police, it was tough, but not impossible to swallow. A classic case of clean and simple political hypocrisy. And while it was unfortunate to see the luster of a promising Jewish politician lose its shine, it certainly didn't seem like all hope was lost for Mr. Spitzer. Jewish mothers could still call their little aspiring politicians 'The next Eliot Spitzer!' without it sounding absolutely disgusting. Then came "Client 9" and the fall from grace that was too epic for even the most delusional parent to ignore.

Will Mr. Spitzer's dalliances and indiscretions prevent Jews from pursuing law degrees? Of course not. We are, if anything, a litigious people. The commandments, the Talmud, every rabbi's laminated and immutable office hours—these aren't just documents, they are inborn laws that somehow we know if we are defying, even if we never formally learned what they are. We *feel* laws every time we have a twinge of regret when biting into a cheeseburger, or looking at the doorframe of a new apartment and thinking, "Ugh, I can't put up a mezuzah. Then everybody in the building is going to know I'm Jewish and it's going to be a whole thing." So it would be foolish to suggest that Mr. Spitzer's wandering shmekl single-phallically clogged up the Jewish lawyer pipeline. Nobody's dreams (or no parent's dreams) of arguing before Supreme Court, and then, of course, serving on it, will be deferred.

On the other hand, it would be understandable if for the time being no Jewish crusader is too keen on stepping into the spotlight of high-profile public litigation or politics. Politicians are always caught with mistresses (compensated or otherwise), and in the years immediately following the Spitzer scandal, nobody made strict, exclusive connections between Mr. Spitzer's downfall and new salacious liaisons that came to light in the political world. There wasn't a unique enough connection. Even when South Carolina Governor Mark Sanford went gallivanting down Argentina way, nobody laid any Spitzer-the-sequel charges on him. Infidelity and politicians is a motif unto itself. But if another Jewish politician were to cheat on his wife? That's deserving of at least five hundred extra trend pieces in the media. It's not the same old politician's-libido-getting-him-into-trouble story, oh no. Now it's that infamous Jewish libido that caused all the mayhem!

"Tonight on *Nightline,* do all Jews cheat on their spouses? And does their religion actually require it? We'll investigate . . ."

"I'm Brian Williams. Our top story: Five states have now passed laws prohibiting all noncastrated male Jews from running for office . . ."

"This is CBS News with a breaking story. Jews are coming for your women."

Obviously a Jewish politician isn't guaranteed to cheat on his or her spouse. It's fairly unlikely, in fact. Surely "hypocrite," "adulterer," and "overall jerk-off" rank high above "Jewish" on the list of adjectives that first come to mind when describing the failed governor. Few Jewish would-be politicians would even think themselves capable of infidelity. Ah, but the neurosis that they are not aware they are capable of pulling a Spitzer? That rampant condition is able to halt the rise of even the fiercest Jewish political animal. Facing the scorn of a constituency you let down by cheating is one thing, but adding the fear you would inadvertently open the floodgates of Jew-hating and the hoots and hollers of "Man, those Yids can't keep it in their pants!" is perhaps enough to kill a Jewish person's political aspirations entirely.

JERRY SPRINGER

Talk Show Host, Future Master of Ceremonies for the Apocalypse

HE DOES MORE THAN WATCH HOOKERS FIGHT ON HIS SHOW

- JD from Northwestern Law, and delivered the school's commencement address in 2008. He's respected by legal minds and the mindless alike.
- Served as the 56th mayor of Cincinnati. You know what they say, first Cincinnati, then the White House.
- Went on *Dancing with the Stars* so that he could learn to waltz at his daughter's wedding. Imagine, a Jewish father doing something at his child's wedding besides eating.
- Won the 2008 Fox Reality Award for Favorite Host for his work on *America's Got Talent*—a feat that will never be replicated again because both the award show and the Fox Reality Channel no longer exist.
- Was a featured speaker at both the United Jewish Israel Appeal in London and the St. Louis Jewish Book Festival. Jews all over the world love hearing him speak even if he's not moderating a debate between neo-Nazi dwarf twins who date each other.

A DISTINGUISHED CAREER IN DESTROYING THE FABRIC OF HUMANITY

- While serving as a Cincinnati city councilman, was busted for paying for and using the services of a Kentucky prostitute. Who knew some of his shows were inspired by events from his own life?
- Winner of the 1999 Razzie Award for Worst New Star for *Ringmaster*. Maybe he shouldn't have made that piece of garbage in the first place.
- Sued after a guest murdered his ex-wife following their appearance on a "Secret Mistresses Confronted" episode. That should have been a hint that it was time to cancel the show, Jerry.
- Once said to Reuters, "I would never watch my show. I'm not interested in it." His show is so bad, even he can't kvell about it.
- Is the host of *The Jerry Springer Show.* Really, what else is there to say?

How does a Jewish politician once called "the best I've ever seen, bar none" by a strategist for Bill Clinton, Michael Dukakis, Jimmy Carter, Ted Kennedy, and Howard Dean transform into a talk show host regularly within twenty feet of people who behave like failed experiments by the good Doctor Moreau? Perhaps only the man himself knows, but it probably has something to do with ratings. For nearly two decades, Jerry Springer has moderated the back-and-forth grunts, shrieks, fisticuffs, and strip-offs of America's worst and dimmest. Why the FCC bothers fining any other show on television is a total mystery. An actual sampling of topics from a recent season includes: "Your Twin Might Be the Father," "The Babysitter Stole My Husband," "Gay Cousins in Love," "Sex, Chicken & Candy!" (you should avoid thinking too hard about how those elements go together), "My Pimp Wants to Marry Me," and the charmingly forthcoming, "I Came Here to Fight!" On the one hand, you could say that Mr. Springer is at least the most sane and intelligent person in the room, but on the other hand, he's still in the damn room. Actually, that makes him the worst person in the room because he, of all people, should have the good sense to step out of it.

What makes seeing a Jewish person lead this daily cavalcade of repugnant dunderheads so vexing is that, no matter how sincere his "Final Thoughts" at the end of each show are, he's still encouraging the racism, sexism, and extraordinary depravity. He wants the bigotry and the blowups, because every time they happen he gets to stand in smug silence as the roaring chant of "Jer-ry! Jer-ry! Jer-ry!" dances its way down his ear canals. Is it too broad to say that it's super-duper bad to hear a Jewish person's name become the de facto soundtrack of the decline of civilization? The association of Jews with a dystopian vision of a future in which an inbred, imbecilic ruling class controls the fate of mankind would be considered a bad one, correct?

As the title of his autobiography and roman à clef movie, *Ringmaster,* attests to, Mr. Springer is the man in charge of the circus, and that self-awareness makes his hosting even more despicable. He's not mistaken or naive in any way; there's no secret good-hearted aim behind the overdose of dreck. *The Jerry Springer Show* is a forum for terrible people to be terrible, and in willfully facilitating it, he promotes whatever insane actions got the guests on the show in the first place. God help us all if the words, "I'm'a cheat on my wife with my sister so I can get on *Springer*" have ever been uttered.

At least other filth-talkers that appear in this book, such as Howard Stern and Michael Savage, can claim they're exercising their first amendment rights, but half of all the words on Mr. Springer's show are either bleeped or indecipherable so that argument is out the window. The notion that he is promoting a dialogue is not a stretch; it's a lie. More meaningful discourse occurs around a cockfighting ring than on the stage of *The Jerry Springer Show*.

In recent years the show has, thankfully, veered away from becoming a regular platform for the KKK and other hate groups and shifted almost exclusively to the three 'in's: infidelity, incest, and indeterminate gender. Maybe Mr. Springer became fed up with extending a courteous invitation to the racists only to be called "Jew boy," "Jew bastard," and "hook nose" on the set of his own show. Giving these hooded cretins a nationally televised soapbox for so many years, however, was an asinine move on Mr. Springer's part that still resonates today. Just because there is freedom of speech, it doesn't mean we have to provide microphones and ad-supported airtime to any backwoods Cletus with an opinion.

It's far too optimistic to believe that Mr. Springer exposed the stupidity of their beliefs. For every viewer who watched and said, "Look at these bigoted morons on TV. What buffoons. I wish I were employed right now so I wouldn't be watching this crap," there was a different viewer who watched some Ku Klux Klan Grand Dragon Wizard Vulcan Tornado Master (or whatever they're called) and said, "Hey, this guy's makin' sense!" Maybe you think it's unlikely anybody would come away with that conclusion? Consider this. The viewer was, in the first place, willingly watching *The Jerry Springer Show*.

LAURA SCHLESSINGER

Giver of Advice, Taker of Dignity

WANT LIFE ADVICE FROM A STRANGER YOU CAN'T EVEN SEE? CALL DR. LAURA

- Hosted third-highest rated radio show in the country and authored 12 pleasantly titled books such as *Ten Stupid Things Women Do to Mess Up Their Lives* and *The Proper Care and Feeding of Husbands*.
- Certified as a marriage, family, and child counselor from USC. Maybe some of her guidance is based on actual training!
- Sells jewelry for charitable causes and raised over $1 million for Operation Family Fund. If only she would spend all her time doing that.
- Awarded the National Association of Broadcasters' Marconi Award for Network/Syndicated Personality of the Year in 1997. See! There are other words to describe Laura's personality besides "petrifying."
- Holds a black belt in martial arts, so she can mess you up verbally *and* physically.

IF YOU THINK SHE CAN HELP YOU, YOU'VE GOT MUCH BIGGER PROBLEMS

- Referred to herself in a *Los Angeles Times Magazine* profile as a "prophet." Let's be nice and call that a stretch.

- Hosted a television show that lasted only a year due to terrible ratings, a 34-city protest, *The New York Post* accusing her of planting members of her staff as guests, and an advertiser boycott. Other than those factors, the show was a rousing success!
- Comments about homosexuals were so abusive that the Canadian Broadcast Standards Council found her in violation of its Code of Ethics. Don't offend Canada! We might have to flee there one day.
- Felt the need to make a big to-do on her show about deciding to no longer practice Judaism. You couldn't just keep that a personal matter?
- Decided to end her radio show in 2010 after earning national scorn for using—eleven times—that one word that starts with "n" that you really, really, really shouldn't say while she was speaking on-air to an African American woman. Then decided to make matters worse by saying, "I want to regain my First Amendment rights. I want to be able to say what is on my mind." Say anything you like, Dr. Laura. Just stand as far away from us as you can when you say it.

Let's say you're hosting a party for some close friends and somebody who you are somewhat acquainted with through a JCC karate class decides to invite herself. There's extra room and plenty of salmon mousse amuse-bouches, so you extend a little hospitality and welcome her into the party. Then the individual proceeds to spend the entire party making off-color remarks, complaining about the other guests, and proclaiming that she wishes she had been invited to your cool Christian neighbor's party—all before leaving by kicking through a window. Such is the relationship between Dr. Laura Schlessinger and the Jews.

The radio-based advice-supplier with a Ph.D. in physiology (oh, did you think the "Dr." in Dr. Laura applied to her career in a relevant way?) converted to Orthodox Judaism in the late nineties after having grown up in a nonreligious home with a Jewish father. Following her conversion, Dr. Schlessinger used Jewish law as the basis for some of her on-air tips about relationships, love, and life, which had disaster written all over it. In a 2000 article in the magazine *The Jewish*

Homemaker, Dr. Schlessinger says, "I always say to callers, according to Jewish law, this is the law; let's see how we can extrapolate to your situation." Boiling down Jewish law into radio-friendly three-minute sound bites meant to help a largely Gentile audience deal with questions like, "What do I do if I'm married but still love my high-school boyfriend?" is not the best way to represent a religion. And if it is, we've been sitting in hours and hours of services for nothing.

Really, rabbis, if there's some miracle shorthand to the proper interpretation and application of Jewish law that you've all been sharing exclusively with Dr. Schlessinger, it's time to start spreading the wealth. Some of us have issues that we would rather not go through a physiology Ph.D. holder with a radio show to sort out.

Anybody who had ever listened to a broadcast of the *Dr. Laura Show* knows the eponymous host delivered her moral teachings from a staunchly socially conservative point of view, and there's nothing inherently wrong with that. Some people like coffee, some people like tea, some people like telling total strangers that they live flawed lives because of the way they were born. Around the time of her Orthodox adventure, however, the rhetoric reached a fever pitch. Dr. Schlessinger wasn't just delivering her oft-referred-to "straight talk" about how wives should blindly do whatever their husbands want for thirty-day stretches or how child day-care centers are really "day orphanages." She was calling homosexuality a "biological error," declaring the homosexual lifestyle "deviant," and saying "a huge portion of the male homosexual populace is predatory on young boys." To be fair, Dr. Schlessinger frequently tried to clarify her comments by saying she had "never called homosexuals errors. [She] called the sexuality an error." So homosexuals themselves weren't the problem. Rather the problem in her mind was the fact that homosexuals . . . were homosexual. Clear?

Not surprisingly, Dr. Schlessinger found that if you make enough blanket statements casting ten percent of the population as aberrations and pedophiles, people tend to get a little miffed. So during Yom Kippur, of all days,—Dr. Schlessinger took out a full-page ad in the entertainment trade magazine *Variety,* apologizing (sort of) for her remarks. Said Dr. Schlessinger, "On the Day of Atonement Jews are commanded to seek forgiveness from the people we have hurt." OK, so she co-opted the holiest day of the year for the purpose of easing a public relations crisis. Strike one. She then justified her statements by saying they were made "from the perspective of an Orthodox Jew and a staunch defender of the traditional family." All right, backtracking and using your religious morals to substantiate opinions that you first claimed to make from a scientific perspective. Strike two. "Many people perceive [the comments] as hate speech. This fact has been personally and professionally devastating to me as well as to many others." Claiming to be the real victim in a situation she both created and perpetuated. Out!

And out she was. Only a few years after she effectively blamed her understanding of Judaism for her condemnation of homosexuality, she announced to her millions of listeners that "my identifying with this entity [Judaism] and my fulfilling the rituals, etc., of the entity—that has ended." Never mind the fact that her interpretation of the Jewish view on homosexuality was hardly a universally accepted one. Never mind the fact that she was hardly a beacon of Orthodox Judaism at the time, once saying of her refusal to cover her hair in public, "The wig thing I'm not up to." Never mind the fact that Jews lambasting minority groups that shared in the suffering of the Holocaust was hardly a sensible or compassionate thing to do. What's really going to fry your knish is that she went on to say, "By and large, the faxes from Christians have been very loving, very supportive. From my own religion, I have either gotten nothing, which is 99 percent of it, or two of the nastiest letters I have gotten in a long time. I guess that's my point—I don't get much back. Not much warmth coming back."

She didn't get much warmth back. Come on, Jews, where were we, huh? A reactionary with only a few years of Jewish education was saying her beliefs were the product of Judaism despite that fact that she held said beliefs long before her conversion and previously maintained they were a matter of scientific fact. Why weren't we jumping up en masse to defend her? No wonder she felt the need to publicly dump and humiliate Jews like we were the ugly girl in high school.

Finally, Dr. Schlessinger concluded her selfish abandonment of Judaism by saying, "I have envied all my Christian friends who really, universally, deeply feel loved by God. They use the name Jesus when they refer to God . . . that was a mystery, being connected to God time and time again." First of all, if you're looking to convert to Christianity, it probably shouldn't be based on envy on account of the whole cardinal sin issue, but that's for them to decide. Second, publicly all but coming to Jesus after enduring a personal and professional mess of your own making is all but saying, "The devil made me do it," only in this case, the "devil" is Judaism. Maybe, though, none of these actions by Dr. Schlessinger should come as a shock. After all, have you heard some of the farkakte advice she gives?

LLOYD BLANKFEIN

CEO of Goldman Sachs and the Only Person Who Made Any Money from 2007 to 2010

HE WORKED HARD FOR HIS MONEY! WE'LL SEE IF A GRAND JURY LETS HIM KEEP IT

- Grew up in the Linden Houses project in Brooklyn. He didn't eat his kasha with a silver spoon.
- A product of public schools who went on to Harvard and Harvard Law. Take that, blue bloods!
- Serves on several charitable, philanthropic, and academic boards. He helps enrich things other than himself, or possibly just helps himself sleep at night.
- 18th on *Forbes*'s list of 2009's Most Powerful People. If he stays out of prison, he might crack the top ten one day!
- *Financial Times* 2009 Person of the Year. #1 out of 6.8 billion!

HOW ABOUT GIVING OUT BONUSES FOR NOT BEING A SHMENDRIK?

- Led Goldman Sachs during a time in which the firm profited off of pretty much every miserable thing to happen in finance, from the American subprime mortgage crisis to the collapse of the Greek economy. Like we need a whole 'nother country angry at us.

- Suggested "apply[ing] basic standards to how we compensate people in our industry" after taking home a compensation package worth $43 million in 2008. Too little, too late, Lloyd.
- Receives anywhere between 75 and 100 pieces of hate mail . . . per day. On the bright side, it appears he hasn't bankrupted people to the point where they can no longer afford stamps.
- Apologized for the financial crisis by saying, "We participated in things that were clearly wrong and we have reasons to regret and apologize for." Hey, that's great. Now how about actually correcting your business practices.
- Named the Most Outrageous CEO of 2009 by *Forbes,* even over Merrill Lynch CEO John Thain, who blew $1.2 million redecorating his office.

The Jewish Banker. Without the stereotype, what would anti-Semites be left to talk about? All of their world-takeover theories would ring so hollow. Are there industries that really are run by Jews? Sure there are, but none of them quite pack the same ominous punch. You can almost hear the Jew-haters now. . . .

"You know how the kikes control the government, don't you? Through the matzoh industry. It's well documented. There are more Jews in the matzoh industry than any other type of person. Just look at any list of the top matzoh CEOs. Jew, Jew, Jew. Anytime they want to pull the strings in Washington, they call up and say 'If you don't do what we want, you're not getting any unleavened bread. We're hiding *all* the afikoman, understand? Don't fuck with us, we're the Jews.' "

So there's a big revelation for you: Anti-Semites don't like bankers who are Jews, and the firm that seemingly caters to their every hysterical belief is Goldman Sachs. Former executives have occupied government positions as high up as treasury secretary (never mind the fact that most of those execs were not Jews), and when the funeral pyre of the global financial system got torched, the investment bank remained unscathed and went laughing all the way to, well, itself.

As chairman and CEO of the firm, Lloyd Blankfein seems to be at once fully cognizant of the delicacy with which a singularly successful company during tough times should carry itself and oblivious as to the correct way to do that. Just before reporting $13.5 billion in earnings, about $40 billion in revenue, and staggeringly high bonuses in 2009, the helmsman of the Bad Ship Goldman tried to endear itself to the public with pitiful, last-minute stunts, such as increasing the size of its charitable foundation and asking top executives not to look like they're having too much fun when they take afternoon money-baths in their monogrammed pools. It's possible, though the chances were admittedly low, that the criticism of Goldman Sachs could have been limited to the facts—that betting against the very chazarai mortgages they bundled or manipulating futures markets in a way that did not reflect actual supply were dubious-at-best, criminal-at-worst business practices that had nothing to do with the religion of its chairman and CEO. Then Mr. Blankfein looked down at his foot and thought, "I wonder if that could fit in my mouth?"

First there were whispers, according to finance reporter Charlie Gasparino, that in August of 2009 people inside the firm felt that Goldman Sachs was only being attacked in the media because of the anti-Semitic perception of the Jewish banker. Right, and John Wilkes Booth only gets a bad rap because everybody secretly hates actors. Jew-haters have probably been maligning Goldman Sachs since Marcus Goldman set up shop on Pine Street, and only now this is a concern? The firm's recent megasuccess most likely gave bigots a shot in the arm, but the charge that there are sleeper anti-Semites in the media waiting for an epic financial catastrophe to pounce is just as demented as conspiracy myths about Jews.

Without a serious journalistic investigation (which suits neither the laziness nor the skill of your author), it's difficult to say how widespread the feeling is inside the company that anti-Semitism in the press was at the root of the criticism. Unfortunately it doesn't matter, because three months later Mr. Blankfein gave an interview to *The Times* in which he signed, sealed, and delivered an invitation to anybody who wanted to tie Goldman Sachs's money-gobbling ways to Judaism. Asked if he saw any cap on the amount of money Goldman Sachs should be raking in, Mr. Blankfein replied that he was a banker "doing God's work."

Oy gevalt.

We might not be able to know the will of HaShem, but it most certainly is not underwriting mergers and acquisitions and collecting $13.5 billion in annual profits. What does HaShem need with cash? Maybe He goes into a store and maybe He sees something He likes—say, a nice reading lamp—but when He gets to the register with the item He can just say, "Listen, I'm taking this nice reading lamp, but don't worry. I'm HaShem. I'm good for it." Mr. Blankfein went from being a Jew who is a banker to being a Jewish banker. You see the difference?

You want to handle money on behalf of God, Mr. Blankfein? Become a comptroller for a synagogue. Unless you want to do that, keep your business over *here* and your religion over *here*. We have enough problems without people thinking Adonai spoke unto Lloyd as he stood atop the Goldman Sachs Tower in Jersey City, "Lloyd! Employee of Goldman! Alumnus of Harvard! Gala chairman of the Rockefeller family's Asia Society! Hear me now as I say unto thee, short the housing market."

SOLOMON DWEK

(ALONG WITH MOSHE ALTMAN, RABBI EDMOND NAHUM, RABBI SAUL KASSIN, RABBI MORDECHAI FISH, RABBI LAVEL SCHWARTZ, RABBI ELIAHU BEN HAIM, LEVY-IZHAK ROSENBAUM . . . A WHOLE LOT OF JEWS IN NEW JERSEY AND BROOKLYN, OK?)

International Ring of Criminal Frums

SOME PARTS OF SOLOMON DWEK'S LIFE DON'T CAUSE AN INSTANT RAGE STROKE

- Served as the vice president of Deal Yeshiva in West Long Branch, New Jersey, where hopefully he never taught an ethics class.
- Gave money to Deal Yeshiva students in need—money that those students might want to consider reporting to the government before they're charged with being accessories to fraud.
- Paid for the hospital and funeral costs of a boy with terminal cancer. This was a mitzvah. He's still a scumbag.
- Funded a memorial statue honoring a Seton Hall University student who perished in a dorm fire. Get the feeling he was just doing nice things to make up for all the terrible stuff he did?
- Donated thousands to renovate a New Jersey local theater, which now can mount a thrilling biographical play about Dwek's life entitled, *Schmuck! The Musical.*

WHAT OFF-BRAND TALMUD WERE THESE GUYS READING?

- Dwek committed bank fraud into the multimillions and even defrauded members of his own family, because those are the kinds of things you can do when you utterly lack a conscience.
- Altman arranged initial meetings so that Dwek could bribe New Jersey mayors and officials. He couldn't have just run for public office like every other a-hole who wants to control municipal business?
- Rabbis Nahum, Kassin, Fish, Schwartz, and Haim laundered millions for Dwek through synagogue-based charities. Have fun hating yourself for wondering whether your own rabbi might be a crook next time you're giving a donation.
- Rosenbaum found guilty of organ trafficking after being recorded by Dwek and an FBI agent. Yes, organ trafficking. Yes, you can be excused if you're feeling nauseous.
- At least a dozen other Syrian and Hasidic Jews implicated in a laundering sting as part of Operation Bid Rig, which Dwek helped the FBI set up. It's like he was inventing ways to betray Jews.

There are certain skills a congregation expects from its rabbinical leadership, such as the ability to give wise counsel and make sense of the world through the teachings of the Torah. Then there are the skills of the New Jersey and Brooklyn rabbis and Jewish community leaders that their congregations likely did not expect, such as the ability to launder millions of dollars, proffer political bribes, and procure a black-market kidney for the low, low price of $160,000.

The case of Solomon Dwek, the corrupt real-estate developer who became an FBI informant after being caught depositing a dud $25 million check one day and withdrawing the funds twenty-four hours later, is so simple that it could've come out of the pages of a highly unsuitable-for-kids Encyclopedia Brown paperback. After he was caught for bank fraud, he turned "cooperating witness" and exposed a money-laundering ring to the FBI in which he'd give bank checks to various charities run by rabbis, who would take a cut and return the rest of the laundered cash to him. Then he used his talents for being an utter rat bastard to bribe mayors and officials in New Jersey. And then, amid all this mishegoss (WARNING: It is advised that you immediately put on a bike helmet or attach some padding to your forehead, because you may involuntarily smack it so hard your palm will crack your skull), Mr. Dwek exposed to the FBI an organ-trafficking operation between Israel and the United States. For the love of God . . .

You want to call a shande on each and every one of these mamzers involved in the scandal, but who the hell do you start with? One could make the case that Mr. Dwek performed a mitzvah by having the courage to bring crooked rabbis and Jewish community leaders to justice, but the only reason he was doing that was to protect his own selfish ass from doing extra-extra-hard time for bank fraud. Then, of course, there is the touchy subject of turning in fellow Jews. Now, it's important to keep in mind that these Jews weren't turned in because they were Jewish, but rather because they were engaging in illegal activity. Even that detail, however, isn't as simple as Alef, Bet, Gimel. In the case of the money-laundering sting, Mr. Dwek would tell the rabbis that he had gone bankrupt and needed the laundered money in order to keep all of his remaining cash from being seized. Now, this excuse doesn't absolve the rabbis by any means, but maybe the pull to help a fellow Jew overruled their better scruples.

Except, fuck no! No! No, no no! And the organ trafficking? What the hell is the rationale there? OK, so somebody's sick in the United States and needs a donor, but taking advantage of people—in most cases, poor Israelis—by paying them for their organs is so despicable, you wonder if the Jews involved were really Jewish at all. Where is the guilt? Where is the relentless, nasal inner voice that asks, "Do you really want to be the one to add unlawful organmongers to the list of trades associated with Jews?"

And this back-and-forth mental game of morality tennis is why the case of Mr. Dwek, along with the rabbis and Orthodox Jewish community members who went down with him, is truly bad for the Jews. The fact that their crimes make Jews everywhere hang their heads in embarrassment is beside the point. They did it, it's done, enjoy prison. Moral turpitude can hit even the most pious among us, and "us" extends to people of every faith. There will be anti-Semites who make the farkakte argument that somehow Judaism, as opposed to basic criminal mania, led to the misconduct, but they beat that drum so often it's just noise to most sensible people. No, the reason it's bad for us is that the juxtaposition of the most religious of our religion doing such awful deeds causes a knee-jerk impulse to stand up for them and attempt to rationalize their motives, which in turn makes us look like the junior varsity turdbuckets to their letterman scumbags.

Jews are like pandas. There's only a couple of us left and there's a natural urge to defend every last one. But a panda that's clawing wildly and foaming at the mouth, no matter how cute and cuddly it is, is still a danger to other pandas. As hard as it is to keep your distance from a fellow panda, do it for your own safety. That's the real message of this book: Whatever you do, stay away from raging pandas.

PHIL SPECTOR

Creator of the "Wall of Sound," Which He Possibly Brags About in Prison

SUCH A GOOD EAR

- Won the Album of the Year Grammy for producing *The Concert for Bangladesh*. To use his talent for a charitable cause is a mitzvah!
- Cowriter of "You've Lost that Lovin' Feeling," which was the twentieth century's most played song on the radio, and that's not even counting drunken bar renditions.
- Produced The Beatles Academy Award–winning *Let It Be*. Something nice to listen to while passing the time in a place like, say, a penitentiary.
- Changed how records were produced with his innovative "Wall of Sound" technique. Glad he was able to do something with his life before deciding to waste it behind bars.
- Inducted into the Rock and Roll Hall of Fame in 1989; a lifetime sentence that he can be proud of!

WALL OF SHANDE

- Produced the 1963 album *A Christmas Gift for You*. Hanukkah songs not good enough for you? Do they embarrass you?

- Rumored to have refused to hand over John Lennon's *Rock 'n' Roll* master tapes. Not such a big deal except for the fact that he supposedly did so with the aid of a gun.
- Ostensibly held ex-wife and Ronettes lead singer Ronnie Bennett hostage inside their home. That's not how you treat mishpocha.
- Might be a matter of taste, but what that man did to the music of Leonard Cohen and the Ramones is unforgivable.
- Not only convicted of second-degree murder, but also acted like a schmuck throughout the trial.

Throughout the 1960s, there was probably no single man who contributed more to the grounding of Jewish teens than Phil Spector. Who knows why young American Jews have so much affinity for rock and pop? Maybe it's because listening to rebellious music is about as close as most of us ever come to rebelling. Maybe it's because nobody under the age of thirty can tolerate the sound of a clarinet in a klezmer band for more than two minutes. Maybe it's because we are just awesome dancers born to move to that sweet rock 'n' roll sound, although probably not. Regardless, as a visionary record producer, Mr. Spector didn't invent pop music, but he was the guy who made it loud. While the list of things Jewish parents absolutely will not tolerate in their homes is an ever-expanding hodgepodge, loudness is always in a vaunted spot, although one would think our parents would appreciate Mr. Spector's Wall of Sound since blasting a song like "Da Doo Ron Ron" provided a wonderful excuse to yell over it. That said, Jewish parents never really need an excuse to yell.

As a little Jewish kid from the Bronx, Mr. Spector was perhaps not the likeliest of guys to revolutionize rock and pop, but he was nothing if not idiosyncratically unique. Musicians like the Ramones, John Lennon, and ex-wife Ronnie Bennett would probably use stronger language than "idiosyncratic" to describe Mr. Spector's eccentricities, but that might be expected of anybody who had a gun waved in their face by a perfectionist, control-freak producer. Indeed, Mr. Spector's predilection for going off the deep end during recording sessions in order to achieve his dream sound was best summed up by the man himself when he referred to his methods as a "Wagnerian approach to rock and roll." What a great model for aspiring Jewish musicians to follow.

"Hey, little Avi, you got a great sound, but if you're gonna make it in the music business, you're gonna have to emulate an anti-Semitic, raving lunatic."

Of course, no matter how bad Mr. Spector is for the Jews, he is very sadly much, much worse for the woman he murdered, so let's be blunt and humorless and say that he is unequivocally a terrible person. In fact, let's make that an across-the-board rule. If you kill an innocent person, you are worse for that individual and that individual's family than you are for a group of people whom you make look bad in the process. Agreed? Great. Glad we could get that out of the way.

Now, having said that, Mr. Spector went to trial every day acting like it was his job to embarrass anybody who has ever had a bar mitzvah. As if being accused of murder wasn't enough, Mr. Spector sat in the courtroom while donning a series of outlandish wigs and often dressing like an elderly background extra in a disco scene from *Saturday Night Fever*. Even convicted football players and gold-digging, drug-addled *Playboy* models know to put on some formal clothes, comb their hair, and not act like an impudent shmegege. The antics made Mr. Spector seem like he was above the opinion of the court, that he would get off simply by virtue of who he was. For a people who are already referred to as "chosen," this brand of arrogant elitism is not one we need on display, especially by somebody who is a total sociopath.

While Mr. Spector could have just been another godless murderer, he instead decided to yank us all into the slammer with him at the last moment. Mr. Spector's wig parade during the trial was not only the result of his insolence, but also of his vanity. It turns out that being accused of murder couldn't humble Mr. Spector, but the public seeing his hairless scalp could. Following his incarceration, he had to dispense with the wigs due to prison policy, so Mr. Spector reportedly pulled out the only legal option that would allow him retain the aesthetic dignity he so did not deserve. He claimed to be an Orthodox Jew and therefore needed to cover his head. By law, the penitentiary had to let him wear a full head–size Breslov kippah. This strategy shows how truly insane Mr. Spector is. He actually believed that he'd gain more buddies in prison by wearing a Jewish skullcap than he would if he revealed his bald head. If you have any compassion for the man, pray that his fellow convicts are big fans of his work on "Unchained Melody."

ORLY TAITZ

Queen of Birthers, Outstanding Interrupter, Dentist

ONLY SOMEWHAT SUSPECT ACCOMPLISHMENTS

- A degree in dentistry from Hebrew University, so at least she is qualified to speak out on the topics of brushing and flossing.
- A JD from Taft Law School, which is nonaccredited, but does have the words "law" and "school" in it.
- Used to have a nonexpired California real-estate license. Surely nobody would mind if she indefinitely postponed a few TV interviews in order to renew that license.
- Claims to have a second-degree black belt in tae kwon do, but why hasn't she shown any recent documentation of this? What is she hiding? Show us the black belt, Orly!
- Has the ability to make the volume on televisions much, much louder no matter how low it is set.

STICK TO DENTAL HYGIENE, PLEASE

- Relentless shouter/questioner of President Obama's citizenship; like the country doesn't have bigger problems to focus on?

- Called people in the media who don't support her allegations "Obama's brownshirts." Really jumped the gun on the Third Reich comparison.
- Alleges that FEMA is building internment camps for "anti-Obama dissidents." Huh. Look at that. A baseless accusation. Perhaps that is indicative of some sort of pattern.
- Ordered to pay a $20,000 fine for misconduct in bringing frivolous lawsuits before the court. A multitalented waster of both time *and* money!
- Probably cancelled a bunch of her patients' checkups in order to shriek on television.

It's always very sad when Jews use their natural, God-given talent to scream at the top of their lungs for boneheaded purposes. If "Let my people go!" is the gold standard of righteous and justified Jewish bellowing, anything that has ever come out of the mouth of Dr. Orly Taitz is the antithesis. Known to most people as the law-acquainted individual (calling her an attorney is an insult to real lawyers, which is no easy task) who leads the charge to have President Obama removed from office because of her belief that he is not a United States citizen, Dr. Taitz is also something of an undocumented polymath, having obtained her dentistry degree, real-estate license, and second-degree black belt. Just for good measure, let's assume she also thinks she's a commercial pilot, a world record holder in the 200 meter sprint, a champion pumpkin farmer, a bronze sculptor, a licensed lion tamer, a forklift operator, and a bowl of soup.

Dr. Taitz's regular habit of bringing frivolous lawsuits challenging Obama's citizenship before the court is probably something we can handle. It's not welcomed, but it's a low-key kind of lunacy and most of the population isn't spending their time riffling through legal briefs looking for crazy lawsuits filed by deranged Jewish lawyers. Unlucky for us, however, putting Dr. Taitz on television makes CNN, MSNBC, and Fox News anchors look like geniuses, so now all of America is privy to this pastel-frocked zealot's inner, inane ramblings that are no doubt the result of peroxide runoff from her hair seeping into her brain. The decision by the cable news channels to put her on screen is understandable, since she is indeed compelling to watch, if only to see if her breathless yelling will culminate in a full sentence (spoiler: it never does).

Of course, news channels now are dominated by shouty say-nothings and plenty of them are Jewish, so what makes Dr. Orly Taitz, Esquire so singularly damning? At the apotheosis of her visibility, Dr. Taitz exploited with abandon what you might call the Holocaust Power Move, wherein a Jewish person uses their personal, historical connection to the horrors of the Nazi era to criticize others, shut down opponents, and support their own hypotheses no matter how ludicrous the claim. Now let's be clear, sometimes the HPM is completely justified and appropriate, but that is exactly why you don't want to overuse it. The HPM is like a hit summer jam. When you first hear it, it's got magnitude. It moves you. But you can't dance to the same song played on repeat. Pretty soon it'll stop resonating. She warned of internment camps that would be built to hold anti-Obama dissidents in the event of his election, and every time she did, everybody took it as the go-ahead to stop behaving like rational adults. She name-called those who questioned her "Obama's brownshirts" with the same casual flippancy as a driver calling a parking-space thief a jerk. She tossed out the insult so effortlessly and so often, there was no way she only reserved such venom for her detractors.

"What are you saying you can't get the stain out? You and your dry-cleaning Hitler youth back there can go to hell!"

"Listen, Goebbels, I did not put *Catch Me If You Can* on my Netflix queue, so I'm not going to send it back."

"Don't come knocking on my door like the SS. I don't care if you are trying to sell me Girl Scout cookies!"

To make matters worse, Dr. Taitz, not surprisingly, is a big fan of propagating the myth that President Obama "was born and raised in radical Islam, all of his associations are with radical Islam," and asks, "Can there be anything scarier than that?" Yes, there is something much scarier than that. Anybody taking Dr. Taitz seriously.

Now, let us examine a proper demonstration of how and when to use the HPM. Do you know who, like Dr. Taitz and her Obama-is-a-Muslim conspiracy buddies, was really good at spreading lies about a people and their religion in order to engender the anger of the masses and divert attention from those truly responsible for the disastrous state of their society? Aw, you already know the answer. Those goose-stepping, sieg-heiling sons of bitches, the Nazis!

For the sake of one of the dumber arguments that has been indulged in modern history, let's say President Obama was a Muslim. Would that, in and of itself, be cause for concern? Granted, some Muslims aren't fans of the Jews (and vice versa), but if we start going down the road of saying all people of a religion feel the same about all people of another religion, that leads us to the ipso facto and ip-so scary conclusion that the bile spewed by Dr. Taitz could come out of any Jew's mouth. It's a great situation if you've ever wanted a dubiously licensed lawyer/dentist/screamer to speak for you, but otherwise, it's pretty bad for us all.

MICHAEL SAVAGE

Jewish Radio Host So Popular Even White Supremacists Can't Help But Like Him!

A PASSIONATE PRACTITIONER OF FREE SPEECH

- A staunch supporter of Israel. As for supporting Jews who don't share his beliefs, not so much.
- Gives generously to charities ranging from legal defense for U.S. Marines to the International Fund for Animal Welfare. He is kind to all species, as long as they're not liberal.
- Winner of the 2007 Freedom of Speech Award from *Talkers Magazine*. Even if what he says is awful, he does use his big mouth to exercise his constitutional rights.
- Ph.D. from the University of California, Berkeley, in epidemiology and nutritional ethnomedicine. Michael, you could be doing such good work in medicine. You should stop this meshuge radio dream and focus on that instead.
- Syndicated in over 300 U.S. markets. Good to know in case you were ever in a situation in which listening to a man scream venom for three hours could save your life.

SOME TERRIFYING WAYS HE'S USED FREE SPEECH

- His cheery view on autism: "In 99 percent of the cases, it's a brat who hasn't been told to cut the act out. That's what autism is. What do you mean they scream and they're silent? They don't have a father around to tell them, 'Don't act like a moron. You'll get nowhere in life. Stop acting like a putz. Straighten up. Act like a man. Don't sit there crying and screaming, idiot.' "
- His kind response to a gay caller with whom he disagreed: "Oh, so you're one of those sodomites. You should only get AIDS and die, you pig; how's that? Why don't you see if you can sue me, you pig? You got nothing better to do than to put me down, you piece of garbage? You got nothing to do today? Go eat a sausage, and choke on it. Get trichinosis."
- His creative proposal to girls in the San Francisco area trying to help the homeless: "[The girls] can go in and get raped by them because they seem to like the excitement of it."
- His contemplative advice to people of the Muslim faith: "Take your religion and shove it up your behind."
- His measured commentary on CNN anchor and fellow Jewish broadcaster, Wolf Blitzer: "The type that would stick Jewish children into a gas chamber to stay alive another day."

Expressing an opinion about conservative radio talk-show host and bestselling author Michael Savage is tricky if you don't have an interest in being sued by him or his syndicator. Individuals and institutions who have found this truth out the hard way include the University of California, Berkeley, the Council on American-Islamic Relations, a British home secretary, and a host of Web sites that call for the removal of his show, *The Savage Nation,* from the airwaves. For a guy who spends the majority of his day slandering everybody from politicians to minorities to parents of autistic children, and fervently defending his First Amendment right to do so before a listening audience of 10 million, his litigious actions against those who would dare speak out against him could be referred to charitably as ironic and hypocritical (and realistically as off-the-rails batshit wackadoo). The man born Michael Weiner speaks from the very tips of the feathers on the right wing. His three-word mantra is "borders, language, and culture," as in close the borders, speak only the English language, and defend an American culture that presumably revolves around listening to his show.

Listening to Dr. Savage is, in a word, confusing. That might seem like a mild way to put it, but that's truly what the experience boils down to if you can make it past the initial urge to douse your radio in gasoline, set it on fire, sweep up the charred remains, divide and bury them in the four corners of the earth, and then salt said corners of the earth so that no new life bearing the taint of Dr. Savage's medium can spring forth.

Where were we? Oh yes, he's confusing.

Hearing a Jewish-American staunchly advocate shutting down his country's borders makes about as much sense as hearing a Native American demand more downy-soft smallpox blankets from the British. Given that Jewish diasporas come along with the same frequency as Halley's Comet, how does a xenophobic immigration policy not inevitably bite us in the ass? In a nationalist vision of America, Jews fit in about as naturally as both illegal and extraterrestrial aliens. Then there is the "language" component of Dr. Savage's ideal America, which he regularly contradicts by sprinkling his monospiels with Yiddish. In fact, on his Web site, in between ads for penny stocks that will turn $200 into $2.1 million and need-to-know news on male potency, Mr. Savage trumpets a banned TV commercial for his show in which he tells viewers twice in a span of nineteen seconds, "Don't be a schmuck." The first English words uttered by the Pilgrims upon disembarking the *Mayflower* may have been lost to time, but they definitely were not "Oy, that was some schlep! Let's have a little nosh. Does anybody know if maize is kosher?" As for his call to preserve so-called American culture, the only rational response is, "Huh?" Who knows what exactly the definition of American culture is, but those who say it's baseball, hot dogs, and apple pie sure as hell don't mean Sandy Koufax, Hebrew National, and charoset on matzoh.

Much of the befuddlement a Jewish listener might experience listening to

Dr. Savage may be a product of his own curious relationship to Judaism. Without disagreement between Jews, we would have almost nothing to talk about, so the fact that he regularly aims his fury at Jews of opposing ideologies is no big shock. However, in the course of demeaning them, he often takes special care to point out that they are a member of the tribe, regardless of relevancy. Between saying that Senator Lieberman was "throwing his bagel into the ring to be president" to addressing the president of the Southern Poverty Law Center as "obviously a Jew from New York" to calling talk-show host Jerry Springer "hook-nosed," you'd not be a nutcase for thinking Dr. Savage earned a spot beside Roy Cohn in the American-Jew Self-Hate Hall of Fame. On the other hand, in light of Dr. Savage titling a chapter in his book *The Savage Nation,* "Christophobia: in Praise of Christianity," changing his last name, and allegedly reporting a radio columnist who identified him as Jewish to the Anti-Defamation League, you'd also not be a nutcase for thinking Dr. Savage is not a Jew, self-hating or otherwise.

Not totally dumbfounded yet? Keep reading! Because Dr. Savage is most definitely Jewish, and when former UK Home Secretary Jacqui Smith banned him from the United Kingdom, he claimed it had nothing to do with the content of his inflammatory opinions and everything to do with his Judaism. Said Dr. Savage in a statement to WorldNetDaily, "Make no mistake about this—they 'chose' me because I am the only talker in the top five who is Jewish! The old anti-Semitic strain has resurfaced in England, not among the right wing, but on the socialist left." Can a Jewish person both slander others with anti-Semitic slurs and at the same time condemn what he perceives as anti-Semitic actions taken against him? Absolutely. Dr. Savage lives in America, baby. He can call a cow a chicken and a chicken his mother. What good is a right to free speech if you don't test its strength by saying the most nonsensical, eyebrow-raising, ass-backward things you can think of? Now is a Jewish person who both slams and expresses anti-Semitism good for the Jews? Probably not, but once again, the answer as it relates to Dr. Savage is confusing.

You see, Dr. Savage's regular bashing of Jews, when blended with his own Jewish identity and his staunch support of Israel (which, in another odd turn, he believes has no greater enemy than the "liberal Jew"), causes a really wonderful and altogether delightful sight: White supremacists having a complete mental breakdown. Not that anybody should read hate-site message boards, but if you do, you should know that viewing a conversation under the headline, "Is Michael Savage Jewish or not? I need to know this," is a joy to behold. You can almost hear the neurological circuitry in their bigoted brains snapping into disrepair. Actual quotes from brokenhearted racists upon learning Dr. Savage is Jewish include, "Man . . . I don't know. I have listened to Savage for so long. I mean, the guy says exactly what I am thinking. And he is so pationate [*sic*] about it—just listen to the man talk to a queer or a black man or a liberal"; "Now I'm an optomistic [*sic*] person and I don't get down on myself, but its honestly going to make me sad if I find I can't trust Savage anymore. The man is my hero"; and finally the somber rumination, "I am kind of confused as to what I should do at this point."

So is a man who causes such angst, consternation, and division in the anti-Semitic community actually good for the Jews? The answer is—you guessed it—confusing. But, hey, if Jews and anti-Semites can feel the same way about a guy, maybe there's hope for peace between the two sides after all.

On second thought, nah. There isn't.

PAUL WOLFOWITZ, DOUG FEITH, AND RICHARD PERLE

Unlicensed Architects of the Iraq War

A GROUP OF VERY INTELLIGENT, HARDWORKING IDIOTS

- All three have devoted most of their careers to public service, minus a few years in which they made some sweet coin through their political connections.
- They have taught or lectured on several university campuses, and occasionally weren't protested by both students and faculty!
- Actual fun nicknames for the trio bandied about Washington include "Wolfie" (Wolfowitz), "The Prince of Darkness" (Perle), and "The Fucking Stupidest Guy on the Face of the Earth" (Feith).
- The trio had a major impact on the prosecution of a war without having one iota of military experience between them. How talented!
- Not, as of yet, found guilty of war crimes. Not so easy when your rationale for military action turns out to be a bunch of dreck.

IF ONLY THEIR CASE FOR WAR WAS STRONGER THAN THE CASE TO HATE THEM

- When asked, "How do you account for the intelligence failures regarding weapons of mass destruction in Iraq?" Wolfowitz responded, "I don't have to." Oy, the God complex on you!

- In an interview with *The Washington Post,* Feith said, "I am not asserting to you that I know that the answer is, we did it right. What I am saying is it's an extremely complex judgment to know whether the course that we chose with its pros and cons was more sensible." No, it's not that complex. Your choice wasn't sensible.
- At a Senate Foreign Relations subcommittee hearing in 2001, Perle stated, "Does Saddam now have weapons of mass destruction? Sure he does . . . How far he's gone on the nuclear-weapons side I don't think we really know. My guess is it's further than we think." Oh wow, that was very, very wrong!
- According to a Pentagon transcript, Wolfowitz said, "The truth is that for reasons that have a lot to do with the U.S. government bureaucracy, we settled on the one issue that everyone could agree on which was weapons of mass destruction as the core reason [for going to war]." Next time, try a reason based in reality.
- Feith told *The New York Times,* "The danger of Saddam's providing WMD to Al Qaeda or another terrorist group—there you had a real problem, because his record on WMD was indisputable." Now was that, "My mother makes the best tsimmis" indisputable, or "I'm too lazy to ask around" indisputable?

The question has been asked many times, specifically by the late singer/philosopher, Edwin Starr. "War, huuuh, good God, y'all, what is it good for?" The answer to the question is simple and unconditional. "Absolutely nothing." But we know that war is not just good, but great for those who like to pin any human suffering on the Jews. Even though anti-Semites have been known to start a war or two or ten, the mere suggestion that a Jew is involved in a military operation can magically turn any snarling blond beast into a pacifist bunny. Surely if hook-noses are involved there must be some dastardly ulterior motive, unlike all those morally just wars waged by everybody else! To these knuckle-dragging gum flappers, former Deputy Secretary of Defense Paul Wolfowitz, former Under Secretary of Defense for Policy Doug Feith, and former Chairman of the Defense Policy Board Advisory Committee Richard Perle were a trio of gift wrapped Bush-era bozos.

Smug, pretentious, profoundly naive, and, much to our collective displeasure, Jewish.

As three of the major architects of the 2003 Iraq invasion, Mr. Wolfowitz, Mr. Feith, and Mr. Perle formed a triumvirate of wrongness. Like many nerdy Jews trying to emulate the cool Gentile jocks at their high school, the three aped the behavior of Secretary of Defense Rumsfeld, President Bush, and Vice President Scattershot by boldly predicting how American efforts in Iraq would cost little in terms of time, blood, and treasure, and pay off big-time. In 2003, Mr. Perle even prognosticated, "A year from now, I'll be very surprised if there is not some grand square in Baghdad that is named after President Bush."

Surprise!

How about a bissel of Jewish self-doubt, boys? Our natural, anxious pursuit of staying out of trouble, passed down from generation to generation, is there for a reason. It's an innate disposition that is a product of our evolution, like thumbs or IBS. It serves as a check against the inordinately harsh reaction to our screw-ups by frothy-faced anti-Semites looking to justify their hatred in any way possible. It's simply astounding that there wasn't a moment in the run-up to war when Mr. Wolfowitz, Mr. Feith, or Mr. Perle didn't turn to each other and say, "Wow, if we're wrong about this, it's gonna turn into a whole blame-the-Jews thing. I mean look at the three of us. It looks like Bush went to a brotherhood meeting at Temple Beth Israel to get foreign policy advice. Let's take a night to sleep on this plan."

OK, so does that mean Jews shouldn't take part in fighting the just cause? Well, yeah, sure we should. Whether it's America, Israel, or an enclave of time-shares in Acapulco, Jews have just as much a right as anybody to defend the security of their land. We just shouldn't be friggin' yutzes about it. There are basic precautions any member of a high-risk scapegoat group should take, such as making sure you're right in the first place. If global conflict is a disease, Jewish politicos should consider gathering verifiable prewar intelligence and building UN coalition support, much like their regularly scheduled colonoscopy and Tay-Sachs screening. Jews can even articulate an unbiased case for war in Iraq and still be members of the Jewish Institute for National Security Affairs and outspoken supporters of Israel, but what they can't be is (A) chief proponents of evidentiary schlock and (B) at all shocked if people start crying Zionist conspiracy in light of "A."

Who knows why in the world Mr. Wolfowitz, Mr. Feith, and Mr. Perle (along with the rest of the administration) wanted so badly to go to war in Iraq? Preemptive defense? Oil? Liberating an oppressed people from tyranny? The greater good? Cheap Tigris riverfront property? The point is, when there are that many Jews in the room, no matter why or how, there's going to be those who believe—wrongly of course—that it's a Zionist cabal. Even if the Iraq War was a rousing success—no casualties, the discovery and safe disarmament of WMDs, a seamless democratic regime change, a swift homecoming for the troops, and even Mr. Perle's utopian vision of Baghdad's George W. Bush Square—there would still be those who write screeds on how it was all a plot by the Zionist cabal. The difference, however, is that if we were successful, the global reaction would be, "Great job! Let's have more plots by the Zionist cabal!"

BERNIE MADOFF

"Investor"

HERE IS WHERE AN ATTEMPT IS MADE TO SAY GOOD THINGS ABOUT THE INDIVIDUAL IN QUESTION

- Uh . . .
- Um . . .
- Hmm . . .
- Maybe . . .
- Oh, forget it.

WHERE TO BEGIN . . .

- Orchestrator of the largest Ponzi scheme in history—meaning he even ripped off the life work of a dead Italian man.
- Currently serving a 150-year sentence for securities fraud. So that's good.
- Actions caused several nonprofit organizations, including Jewish charities, hospitals, and scholarship funds, to endure major financial setbacks or shut down entirely. Sometimes it's too bad we don't have one of those fancy Christian Hells for people like him.
- At least 2 deaths—one suicide, one heart attack—are alleged to be related to Madoff's misdeeds. May they haunt him as dybbuks! Feh!

- Had a 20-year affair with a former CFO of Hadassah while also fraudulently investing the organization's endowment. If only he had diversified his clients' portfolios as much as he diversified his immoral acts.

Well, here we are. Bernie Madoff. An A+, all-star poster boy for Jews who are bad for the Jews. A modern-day Robin Hood who forgot about the giving-to-the-poor part. With absolutely no moral quotient to serve as a check against his appetite for wealth, Mr. Madoff reinvented what it means for a man to screw others for the shallowest of reasons. It was all about money. There was no Machiavellian ends justifying the means, no good intentions that went awry, no complicated hostage situation where he was forced to illicitly raise billions of dollars to free a beautiful princess but he couldn't tell the cops about it or else her captors would kill her. He wanted dough and he couldn't give two nickels who he hurt in the process. In fact, he probably stole the two nickels that he couldn't give. One wonders how he even had the time to drain investors dry and still maintain his busy schedule of purchasing new yachts and homes and pretending to be a human being with a soul. The true numerical value of his fraud may never be known, but given that $18 to $50 billion is considered "in the ballpark," why even bother using numbers since "a shit-ton" feels far more accurate?

Though victims of the notorious Ponzi schemer came from many walks of life, Mr. Madoff preyed on his own people with a voraciousness that would make cannibals blush. He embedded himself in the Palm Beach Jewish community and picked off nearly a third of the largely Jewish membership at the Palm Beach Country Club. He stole from Jewish charities and organizations ranging from Yeshiva University to the Elie Wiesel Foundation by fraudulently investing their endowments (NB: In the Madoffian language, the verb "to invest" is translated into English as "to rob your tokhes blind"). About the only thing he didn't rip off from his clients was their silverware, which is a good thing because that's what most of them have to sell off now in order to afford groceries.

The technical name for the crimes Mr. Madoff perpetrated against Jews is affinity fraud, although it's tough to see where the affinity enters into it. It probably goes without saying, but usually when we mention somebody is bad for the Jews, it means they have made us look bad or have done something that will end up making life more difficult for us. It's a roundabout way of sticking a fellow Jew in a bad situation, like somebody who comes over for stuffed cabbage night and doesn't use an air freshener before you're about to use the bathroom. They haven't taken a dump right on top of you, they've just stunk up the place. Rarely do we see a Jew who is directly harming a vast number of Jews in material or mortal ways because that, fortunately, doesn't happen too often. Mr. Madoff, though, went after Jews with a kind of focused malice normally reserved for guys with shaved heads and tattoos of an ancient Indian symbol set at forty-five-degree angle.

Whenever a Jewish person seemingly turns on other Jews, there's the tendency to label the individual as self-hating, but here again we find the ganef, Mr. Madoff, was on a much higher echelon of schmuckiness. He didn't hide his Judaism or lead a hateful crusade against Jews. Such activities don't typically attract the kind of savvy, monied investor a hotshot stock broker needs unless he's trying to get Mahmoud Ahmadinejad as a client. Instead, Mr. Madoff sat on the boards of some of the very Jewish institutions whose money he swindled, he gave upward of millions of dollars every year to Jewish charities, and he was, for all intents and purposes, an upstanding mensch that all Jews could hold in high regard. In other words, just as he took on the persona of a money manager who knew what the fuck he was doing, Mr. Madoff took on the persona of a good Jewish boy. Mr. Madoff took strong Jewish moral fiber, wove it into a cheap suit, put it on, and asked our people, "So how do I look?"

Though there are a multitude from which to choose, this particular aspect of his sham was possibly the putz's most damaging, Semitically speaking, and the consequences of the ruse extend far beyond the bank accounts of Mr. Madoff's Jewish clients. When Jews can't trust a man who basically encased himself in a veneer of Jewish goodness, who can we trust? What other previously unthinkable forgeries of Jewish life are out there? Maybe your bubbie's macaroons actually come from a grocery store—and not even a Jewish grocery store but one of those bullshit Passover displays supermarkets put up at the end of an aisle. Maybe your Hebrew schoolteacher was spending all the money you collected for Trees for Israel on Christmas presents for his secret shiksa girlfriend. Maybe all those hours spent in local Hadassah meetings were really viral marketing attempts to sell you galoshes and scented bath soaps. Life is hard enough without having to be concerned that your esteemed brethren are really sleeper-schmucks lying in wait, biding their time for the perfect moment to completely ruin your life. That's the legacy Mr. Madoff has left behind, and it's one that might last long after he stops rotting in prison and starts rotting in a new, subterranean location.

MADONNA

Famed Pop Singer, Not a Jew

NOBODY IS SAYING SHE'S NOT A GOOD PERSON . . .

- Multitalented artist who has sold over 300 million records over a career that has spanned 30 years. If we could honestly claim her as one of our own, we definitely would, uh, consider doing that.
- Named by *Guinness Book of World Records* as the top-selling female recording artist of all time. Also could've been named most successful faux Jewish person of all time.
- Golden Globe winner for her role in *Evita*. She's not Argentine either, by the way.
- Contract with Live Nation for $120 million was one of the biggest in history. Maybe she can spend some money on a public awareness campaign to let people know she's not Jewish.
- Patron of Children of Peace, a organization dedicated to bringing children of Israel and Palestine together to promote understanding and peace. Hey, we'll take the help.

. . . SHE'S JUST NOT A GOOD *JEWISH* PERSON

- Called herself "an ambassador for Judaism" while in Israel. No you're not! Why are we even having this conversation?!

- Champion and popularizer of Kabbalah—as if anybody was asking her to do that.
- Wrapped her arm in tefillin in the music video for "Die Another Day." Guess that means Jews can start casually wearing pope mitres and nobody will mind, since apparently that kind of thing is no longer unbelievably offensive.
- Took on the Hebrew name Esther. She just did. No conversion, no rite of passage, no nothing. Simply woke up and thought, "I'm taking a Hebrew name."
- Appeared on the Jewish newspaper *The Jewish Daily Forward*'s annual list of 50 prominent Jews in 2004, so looks like we're not helping, either.

Dear Madonna,

Enough already! You're not Jewish!

You want to convert? Fine. No one is saying you should, but if you want to, go for it.

Otherwise, stop with the fake Judaism already. You're confusing people!

"La Isla Bonita" is a nice song though.

Thank you.

SCOTT SHERMAN

Idiot

HE HAD SUCH POTENTIAL

- Delivered a very nice speech at his bar mitzvah. There is, of course, a videotape of the event.
- Received decent grades in high school and college. Not what you would call a straight-*A* student, but not an outright embarrassment to his parents.
- Played Broadway songs on piano for his mother anytime she asked even though he really, really, really didn't want to.
- Dedicated *Bad for the Jews* to his parents. This one is a good boy!
- Had an extremely difficult time coming up with positive qualities about himself. So modest!

WHO ASKED FOR YOUR OPINION?

- Never even met any of the people in *Bad for the Jews,* yet he criticizes them like he's some sort of expert. And you expect readers to pay money for this book? The nerve!
- One of "those" Jews who typically only attends services during the Days of Awe.
- Never went on his Birthright trip. You were too busy with your filthy writing to visit the land of your people?

- Dedicated *Bad for the Jews* to his parents. As if they wanted to be associated with this crap!
- Probably went way too easy on himself when listing his negative qualities.

What kind of shmendrik writes a book called *Bad for the Jews*? Is he in any way qualified or authorized to make judgments about who is good or bad for the Jews? Does he think he's doing Jews a service by writing the book? Some nice publisher gives this pisher, Scott Sherman, an outlet to express himself and what does he do with it? He pokes fun at his own people. That's not something you do publicly! That's something you do in the privacy of your own home, along with sex, arguing, and shamefully stuffing your face with crackers at about 4:00 P.M. on Yom Kippur.

For the sake of argument, let's say that writing a book about Jews in the public eye who have committed misdeeds or have generally embarrassed the Jewish people wasn't the absolute worst thing Mr. Sherman could have done with his time. Much in the way that the only person a Jewish mother permits to scold her child is herself, it's better that one of us takes these no-goodniks to task so it doesn't look as if we condone their behavior. But even accepting that premise, a few Jews profiled in this book aren't even that bad! They are ostensibly good people who have shared their considerable talents in meaningful ways; Mr. Sherman kvetching about them only reinforces the stereotype of Jews as nitpickers who could be eating a five-star meal that gives the diner everlasting health and still find a way to complain about the heaviness of their fork.

Weren't there other, more appropriate subjects Mr. Sherman could have picked on? Henry Kissinger made Jews look like bomb-happy hawks who liked to do their dirty work under a thick cloak of secrecy. He wasn't worse for the Jews than some reality show yenta? That comedienne with the foul mouth, Sarah Silverman, couldn't get a talking-to in your little book, Mr. Sherman? You had time to berate Frank Gehry for giving the world some of its most beautiful structures, but there was no room for those despicable people who commit tax fraud, kidnapping, or murder in America and then flee to Israel in the hopes of declaring sanctuary?

What Pritzker Prize–winning buildings did they design to earn an exemption from a tongue lashing?

Mr. Sherman's questionable sourcing for the so-called facts in this book will probably do little to change the minds of those who believe Jews only exist to spread misinformation. Sure, he did his best to present truthful details about those profiled, but he's not an academic researcher; he's just some dreck writer with an Internet connection. How can anything written in *Bad for the Jews* be trusted if the information came from the same cyberrealm that hosts Web sites singularly dedicated to propagating myths about, and hatred of, Jews? Children in Hebrew school may use this book to do a report on a famous Jewish personality, Mr. Sherman! If they get a bad grade because they cite unintentionally inaccurate information in *Bad for the Jews,* it's on your head!

Speaking of anti-Semites on the Internet (in addition to the anti-Semites too illiterate to read or write on online message boards), Mr. Sherman is practically fueling their hateful fire with *Bad for the Jews*. Because certainly if an anti-Semite is looking for reasons to hate well-known Jews, the first place he or she will naturally turn for information on them is a tongue-in-cheek book penned by a Jewish writer. Then again, anti-Semites might not trust the information because it was written by a Jew, which could cause a reverse psychological effect that makes them think some Jews in the book might actually be good people, which would in turn make their whole nonsensical worldview seem really goddamn stupid. Is that bad for the Jews? Absolutely! Think about how moronically anti-Semites already act; now imagine what these birdbrained bigots will do when they're confused to boot. It'll be like throwing a blanket over the head of a rabid dog. They'll chaotically zigzag around, blindly knocking over anything in their path, until they finally slam into a wall and crack their heads open. Then we'll get blamed. Oh, it'll be awful.

And can anybody explain why Mr. Sherman is even included in this book? Maybe he thinks that because he's Jewish it automatically entitles him to a place in this pantheon of artists, entertainers, thinkers, business leaders, and politicians. Talk about your overblown sense of Jewish exceptionalism. Forty-nine entries—all of them documenting noteworthy, prominent people. Then you get to number fifty and it's some putz nobody has ever heard of. Way to end your book with a thud, Hemingwaysteinowitz. The least this scribbler could have done is included a blank page in place of this ego trip. That way readers could tear it out and save money on paper when they write angry letters telling Mr. Sherman how bad *he* is for the Jews. What a schmuck.

ACKNOWLEDGMENTS

During the course of writing, I can, at times, become quite the ornery wretch. I'd like to think there is something charming about the condition, but my more objective self knows that is probably not true. These are the people who nevertheless have supported me, bravely, throughout the writing of this book. Please join me in thanking them:

To Rebecca, my love, you're stuck with me! Isn't that great? I think it's great. Thank you for sharing your life with me. I promise to make it fun.

To my parents, Beryl and Leigh, thank you for refusing to let me entertain the safe choices in life. They're boring and wrong and I'll have no part of them. Thank you.

To Victoria Skurnick and everybody at Levine Greenberg, thank you for advocating, advising, defending, and listening. You make a writer feel like he's got a shot.

To Karyn Marcus and Tom Dunne, thank you for giving me the opportunity to let the, shall we say, unorthodox thoughts in my head escape into the wild.

To Andy Friedman, thank you for bringing your mighty drawing tools to the pages of this book. You are a makeup artist who conceals deftly the blemishes in my writing.

To my trusted readers, Joe Garden, Janet Ginsburg, Todd Levin, Sam Means,

Chris Pauls, Bob Powers, and Anita Serwacki, thank you for the keen eyes when I was too sleep-deprived to see straight.

To Greg Walter and Dianne McGunigle, thank you for allowing me to go off on my literary adventures when I should be focusing on writing that involves smash cuts.

To Stephen and everybody at *The Colbert Report,* thank you for taking me in from the cold and letting me write alongside the most talented people in television. I don't know why you ever let me in the building, but I'm forever grateful that you did.

To all of my friends, relatives, teachers, and mentors, thank you for admitting you know me, even when it's kind of embarrassing.

To Ella, you are a dog. How are you reading this? What else can you do that I don't know about? Anyway, thanks for curling up next to me and letting me bounce jokes off of you.

ABOUT THE AUTHOR

Scott Sherman is a staff writer for *The Colbert Report* on Comedy Central. As part of the comedy-writing collective Action 5, he coauthored *The Dangerous Book for Dogs,* which has been translated into ten languages, *The Devious Book for Cats*, and *The New Vampire's Handbook: A Guide for the Recently Turned Creature of the Night* (all from Villard/Random House). He has been a writer on *Important Things with Demetri Martin*, a consulting producer on the Emmy-nominated *The Simpsons: 20th Anniversary Special—In 3-D! On Ice!*, a contributing writer for *The Onion Sports Dome,* and a writer for the online Onion News Network. In print, he was a contributing writer for *The Onion* and wrote a short story for *The New York Times Magazine*. He is a graduate of the University of Chicago and lives in New York with his wife, Rebecca, and his dog, Ella.

ABOUT THE ILLUSTRATOR

Andy Friedman is an artist and songwriter whose work appears regularly in *The New Yorker, GQ, New York* magazine, and various other newspapers and magazines around the world. He lives with his wife and two children in Brooklyn, and delivers an abundance of his assignments from hotel rooms while on tour in support of his music.